D0062806

OUTSIDE HOLLYWOOD

Happy 13th Birthday, Sanford! May God use your gifts and talents for His glory in His great Kingdom Work. And may you always be an open, empty and willing vessel in His hands.

We love you!
The Popes

2010

Other Books *from* Vision Forum

OUTSIDE HOLLYWOOD

The Young Christian's Guide to Vocational Filmmaking

ISAAC BOTKIN

VISION FORUM *Ministries*
SAN ANTONIO, TEXAS

WWW.OUTSIDE-HOLLYWOOD.COM

FIRST PRINTING
COPYRIGHT © 2007 VISION FORUM MINISTRIES
All Rights Reserved

"Where there is no vision, the people perish."

Vision Forum Ministries
4719 Blanco Rd., San Antonio, Texas 78212
www.visionforum.org

ISBN-10 1-933431-20-2
ISBN-13 978-1-933431-20-8

PRINTED IN THE UNITED STATES OF AMERICA

*For my Father, who taught me everything in this book
and my Mother, who taught me how to write this book*

Contents

THE WARRIOR'S PROFESSION

The movies have been crowbars that Hollywood's humanists have used for a generation to pry Americans away from their first principles: religious, moral, and cultural. —Gary North

Here's a thought that will help you keep the "dream industry" in the right perspective: *Film is a religious weapon.*

I think this is why I like movies. They can be explosively emotional, intellectually startling, and morally stimulating. They can change lives for the better. Or they can lay waste the minds, souls, and even bodies of millions.[1]

---

1. Soviet leader Leon Trotsky had this to say about cinema: "This weapon, which cries out to be used, is the best instrument for political propaganda ... which cuts into the memory and may be made a possible source of revenue." *Pravda,* July 12, 1923.

This is why I treat the filmmaking industry cautiously. Hollywood's once-top-earning screenwriter, Dalton Trumbo, said his profession was "literary guerrilla warfare." He knew, and you must know, that the successful people in this business are warriors. The leaders in this industry are fighting diligently for ideas they want to bring to the screen. Many fight ruthlessly, and can fight pretty dirty, using the weapon of media to inflict cruelty and harm on the ignorant.

Can this weapon be used to fight clean? Of course. But any effective weapon is sharp. Pick up the wrong end, and you will cut yourself to pieces. It is not a plaything or a hobby. If you are not careful, the films you see will hurt you. If you're not discerning, the films you make could harm others. But if you're wise, you could use the most powerful media weapon to annihilate dangerous ideas that have injured entire cultures.

The purpose of this simple book is to help you prepare yourself to be fit for the top position in the industry, that of writer/producer/director. The first thing you need to know is that you can't be a spiritual or moral infant in this business, at any level.

Media educates, and all education is religious. This is why all media is religious communication. Every movie you've ever seen is a treatise of religious doctrine with a religious worldview. Your spiritual convictions and theology must be mature and biblically correct, or you will blindly imitate the *false* theology that presently dominates the industry.

The second thing you need to know is that the industry is changing, providing you more opportunities to enter as an "independent," not beholden to domineering studios, banks, or distributors. This means you can be your own boss, not an apprentice or wage-slave to those who make bad films. This is all the more reason to prepare yourself to draw your own sword and fight wisely for your own projects.

The third thing you need to know is that your family may be your greatest asset in developing yourself as a successful filmmaker. How is your relationship with your family? Are you letting your family environment help you perfect the character qualities that will make you strong, mature, and able to stand responsibly as a professional warrior in enemy territory?

I'm an observer who has seen part of the industry from the outside and then part of the industry from the inside, and I've had a few hard knocks as an adolescent making the transition from outsider to insider. My skills and observations are by no means up there with those of film veterans, scholars, or film historians. But what I've seen has a familial orientation and may help you chart a course that can make you successful emotionally, professionally, and spiritually.

Chapter 1

PILGRIMS AND THE CINEMATIC ARTS

The Ten Commandments are not laws. They are the law. They are not arbitrary regulations like the traffic laws or the election laws or tax laws. Rather they are like the laws of chemistry or physics—an expression of the Divine Mind of the Creator. That is why I have called them the great charter of human relations. —Cecil B. DeMille [2]

This book is not a handbook for producing movies.[3] This book is a sort of production handbook on producing *yourself*—making yourself ready for the more important demands of independent filmmaking. Notice the word

---

2.   Quoted by Ted Baehr in *The Media-Wise Family* (Colorado: Chariot Victor, 1998), p. 147.

3.   The actual technical side of filmmaking is relatively straightforward and it will be easy to find a number of up-to-date books on the subject that will instruct you on the finer points of every technical aspect of filmmaking.

"independent." By that I mean truly independent from the ideas and culture of the film industry, not simply the anti-establishment rebelliousness of the so-called "indie" film movement.

The demands on a film professional who tries to make it outside of Hollywood are more rigorous than the demands on the insider. This book is written for the capable, vigorous outsider.

It's my opinion that in the future, the good films will be made outside of Hollywood, and probably outside of the mainstream "indie" movement. Also the successful films, the creative films, the original films, the financially efficient films, and the moral films. It is also my opinion that "inside" filmmakers compromise too much when in Hollywood. Their souls, for one thing, would fare better outside.[4]

Other filmmakers share my opinion, and a fascinating crisis is developing inside Tinsel Town. Hollywood execs are complaining about "runaways." These are not teenage emigrants who are looking for a real life in the Dream Factory; runaway productions are movies being made outside of Hollywood. Runaways have existed since the late 1940s, but their numbers increased during the '90s. According to a 1999 study commissioned by the Directors Guild of America and the Screen Actors Guild,

---

4. It was Marilyn Monroe who was credited with realizing that, in Hollywood, "they will pay you $50,000 for a kiss, and fifty cents for your soul."

runaways have increased from 14 percent of total U.S. film and television productions in 1990 to 27 percent in 1998. Reports *YaleGlobal*, runaways "have a total negative economic impact of over $10 billion a year" on the Hollywood monopoly.[5]

Today, the practice has reached what the *Los Angeles Times* calls "epidemic" levels. The Los Angeles Economic Development Corporation predicts that more than five thousand Hollywood film jobs will go outside Hollywood by 2005.

DON'T CRY FOR HOLLYWOOD

This is big news for Hollywood because its influence has been so large for so long. This is significant news for you because it means you don't have to run away to Hollywood to be an influential filmmaker. Instead, you can make your own runaway films and contribute to the further decline of Hollywood's monopolistic reign. Outside Hollywood.

Do you really want to witness the decline of Hollywood, and possibly be a party to its demise? Yes, unless you truly prefer trashy movies and disintegrating societies.[6] In that case, Hollywood could use your gifts and talents to further

5. Christina Klein, "The Hollowing-Out of Hollywood," *YaleGlobal*, April 30, 2004.

6. The term "trashy movies" was made popular by Hillary Clinton in a 1994 press statement in which she said, "I want people to know me for what I am. I do use obscene four-letter words (but I am trying to quit), and sometimes Chelsea and I go upstairs and watch trashy movies." *Paul Harvey News & Comment*, March 3, 1994, WISN Radio, Milwaukee.

expand its depressing, destructive mediocrity. Hollywood will readily take what you offer, and give you little but regret in return. But if you agree, instead, with Michael Medved that the "dream factory" is really a "nightmare factory," you'll be better off joining the thousands who are building a better film industry, *and a better film culture*, outside of Hollywood.

This book is about how the industry can work outside of Hollywood—with new rules, new perspectives, new content, new technology, and a completely different kind of success that's driven by completely different kinds of priorities by pioneers who have a rugged kind of maturity. Have you got what it takes to be a pioneer? Can you succeed as a pilgrim in the arts?

This book will list some things you must consider as you prepare for a filmmaking vocation. You need to think about mastery of the craft, and that includes more than just shooting and editing. You will need to think about academic subjects like literary history and the "grammar" of film. You will need to think about complex theological matters, and what God thinks about your career moves. You will need to master a much more responsible worldview than the one you hold today. You must think even more diligently about mastery of yourself.

Do you have the character to be professional in the virtuous sense of the word? Do you have the character to be a leader and not a follower? Do you have the ability to teach yourself everything you need to know—those things which will never be available to you in any school? Can you master an accurate biblical worldview? Can you develop the discernment you need to make difficult decisions about controversial content?

There is good news in this book and there may be some things you do not want to hear. The good news is that there is a meaningful place of leadership for you in the film industry outside of Hollywood. The bad news is that it is a dangerous place. Some warnings are in order.

STANDARD PROTECTION AND STANDARDS PROTECTION

The inherent dangers of filmmaking are similar both inside and outside of Hollywood. Do you think you could maintain enough integrity and independence to create mature and successful films of your own? This book will attempt to help you make the best possible decisions in light of the spiritual intensity of a morally demanding vocation. Because I had the providential opportunity to compare film history with biblical truth from a young age, this book will reference that truth as the standard by which the wisest decisions can be made.[7] Don't ever be ashamed of the fact that the Bible is your only standard of life and conduct. Biblical wisdom is your best protection against futility and error.

---

7.   Ephesians 6:10-24. This book contains many strong personal convictions. These convictions are my own. Don't use any of those convictions to build a case against your conscience or against parental advice.

If you think you're supposed to be in film, you might be right. But you could make a big mistake by jumping in too early. When you make films, you will be thrust into situations requiring extensive moral planning, snap moral decisions, and difficult moral judgments. The business involves far more than being good with a script or handy with a camera. You must train yourself to be wise in ways that few other professions demand wisdom. You must evaluate yourself in spiritual terms. If you're on the right side of spiritual truth, then read on. You're in the right place to take the next step, but you must know the work will still wear you out because fighting the good fight is a *fight*. Which side are you on? Do you have one foot in one camp and one foot in the other? If you're on the outlaw side of spiritual truth, which means you don't care about God's highest standards of right and wrong, this vocation will grind you down to its lowest common denominator.

Even if you are at peace with God and are attentive to scriptural instruction, a career in media will not be easy. It will demand everything from you. It will thrust you into the path of conflict. In fact, your life will read like a tense, dramatic script. As you will learn in this book, all good scripts are based on conflict of a moral variety. In your personal life-story, you will be the protagonist. The main character. The word "protagonist" means combatant or champion. What are you championing? Do you know enough about what you want out of life that you can write an outline of your life's work and then produce what you've written? Could you write a script about your life's work that is truly heroic? Can you then live up to the story?

The lives of even successful modern filmmakers are not necessarily happy. Few film careers have happy endings. Marriages break up early, and not just among celebrities. Many film-crew workers live lonely lives between projects and endure long periods of boredom between stressful production days.

Filmmaking will stress you, tempt you, tire you, assault you, and test you to the very limit. You'll be in moral jeopardy. You will have enemies of the most vociferous kind. One of your worst adversaries may be your own flesh. This is not a vocation in which one easily "escapes sinning," as Puritan Richard Baxter put it. If you are not well on the way to conquering and subduing those internal conflicts that wage war against your soul, stop right now before you think about filmmaking any longer. You would be better to change your mind and your plans before you incur strict judgment on yourself by teaching the wrong things through the world's most powerful teaching and entertainment medium.

THE COMPLEX RESPONSIBILITIES OF ENTERTAINING

Aspiring filmmakers must understand that the film industry is, above all else, show-biz. It is entertainment. The tendency when being exposed to entertainment is to sit back and enjoy, whether one is a student, industry exec, or casual customer.

This book is not entertainment, so please sit up and take these preliminary warnings seriously. If you are going into the world of media, you are entering a jungle of perversities. These are the cold, hard facts about our grossly apostate age. Film is a corrupt industry that sits at the apex of a corrupt culture. The industry is ugly with pagan sophistication that has been dressed up to hide the hostile ideas, seductive error, confusing language, and dangerous experiences of Tinsel Town, which filter into the general culture with every media broadcast or film screening, drowning all in a universal pessimism that influences ugly fashion, meaningless art, perverse architecture, dishonest politics, and brutish music.

To participate in the industry, filmmakers will not only brush up against perversity; they must traffic in highly sophisticated literary, visual, and dramatic arts.

Christian filmmakers must not only be theologically wise and morally stable, but fully familiar with the grammar of film and literary devices, many of which pose supplementary hazards. Filmmaking is no place for spiritual and moral adolescents or thrill seekers. Before you even defend the projects you choose to do, you need to be able to defend your very decision to get into this ugly business. You will need to defend your decision, even to other Christians, some of whom think that the dramatic arts are off-limits to Christians, and will oppose and criticize your work and your choice of occupation. If you can't defend your decisions morally and scripturally, you are in a dangerous place. Test yourself with the following questions:

PILGRIMS AND THE CINEMATIC ARTS

IS FILM A LEGITIMATE MEDIUM FOR CHRISTIANS?

First question: "*Is filmmaking a legitimate medium for Christians to serve Christ and advance His kingdom?*" Put another way: "*Is filmmaking inherently sinful or unwise?*" Is it "*dirty?*"

The dramatic arts have been considered problematic by Christians at least since the fourth century.[8] Augustine said, "stage plays are the most petulant, the most impure, impudent, wicked, unclean, the most shameful and detestable atonements of filthy devil-gods." The Council of Arles (A.D. 314) produced a law that excommunicated actors. Church father Tertullian (circa A.D. 200) argued that acting was sinful because role-playing and play-acting was lying—the dishonest portrayal of another person.[9]

According to Lloyd Billingsley, the Puritans did not object to drama as drama, but strongly criticized the abuses of the theater. William Rankin produced a treatise titled, *A Mirror of Monsters, wherein is plainly described the manifold Vices and spotted Enormities that are caused by the infectious sight of Plays, with the descriptions of the subtle slights of Satan in making them his instrument.*[10]

---

8. K.L. Billingsley, *The Seductive Image* (Crossway Books, 1989), p. 33. Billingsley quotes Percy Scholes, "There was never a moment from the fourth century downwards when some or other leaders of the Church were not fulminating against the stage."

9. Ibid., p. 34.

10. Ibid., p. 35.

These critics were no spiritual slouches. Many of their concerns were absolutely valid and certainly applicable to today's entertainment culture. These godly men witnessed severe cultural and spiritual erosion, caused directly by culturally powerful dramatic arts. They recognized that there has always been a tendency for people in the dramatic arts to tend toward moral lawlessness. The seductive and dominant influence of motion pictures is no less powerful today.

However, the answer to the lawlessness and immorality of the secular entertainment industry is not merely to withdraw from it, but to replace it altogether. Our mission is not to syncretize with paganism, to integrate into their system, or to build upon unrighteous foundations, but to reform our thinking and advance Christian culture God's way.

Additionally, we must reject the error of syncretism which seeks cultural influence by blurring the distinction between Christianity and other religious worldviews.

For my part, I reject the idea that film technology is inherently evil. I believe it is a tool. I further affirm my own belief that the Lordship of Christ applies to every area of life and thought, such that culture is a legitimate realm of work through which the Christian is called to proclaim the glories of Christ. In fact, whether Christians admit this or not, the Christian's interaction with culture is inescapable. We will either seek to build our culture for the glory of God, or we will allow pagans to define culture for us. Along the way, it is biblical to wisely make use of the technology and vehicles for aesthetic communication which God makes available to us. Few are as powerful as the medium of film. Consequently, the issue is not *if* filmmaking is legitimate, but *how* we should legitimately make films.

TO WHAT EXTENT DOES THE BIBLE INFLUENCE MY FILMMAKING?

Once you have reasoned from Scripture that film is a legitimate field, the first question for every Christian filmmaker is this: "*By what standard will I perfect my craft, develop my worldview, and execute my mission?*"

The answer is this: The standard is not Hollywood. The standard is not our present culture. The standard is not our feelings. Nor is the standard our personal experience. The standard is God's Word.

The Bible teaches in 2 Timothy 3:16-17[11] that God's Word is sufficient for all of faith and practice. The glorious doctrine of the sufficiency of Scripture means that within the Bible are all the principles, precepts, and patterns necessary to build worldview and help to make wise decisions in every area of filmmaking.

The Bible may not be a textbook on filmmaking, but it certainly is a source book without which we have no grid for wise decision-making. Of course, the alternative to the authority of Scripture is the autonomy of man.

11. 2 Timothy 3:16-17 "All scripture is given by inspiration of God, and is profitable for doctrine, for reproof, for correction, for instruction in righteousness: That the man of God may be perfect, thoroughly furnished unto all good works."

Either God speaks to these areas and He is sovereign, or man and his personal opinions are sovereign. The latter view is the essence of the very humanistic worldview which has destroyed Hollywood.

THE COURAGE OF YOUR CONVICTIONS

The Bible says that whatever is not of faith is sin. For our purposes ,this means that if you cannot defend an action biblically—don't do it. If you have reservations about your convictions, or doubt that you have the moral certitude to stand up in a field dominated by pagans, don't go into film just because others are doing it.

Define your own theology of media and your own rhetoric of film, based on your own scriptural study. In answering difficult questions about filmmaking, we must never resort to flippant responses or embrace shallow opinions. Face the tough questions head-on with your Bible. It was given not to confuse us but to guide us. My answers to the tough questions in this chapter are my personal responses to serious questions that have required study on my part. I stand by them, but you must still study them out for yourself. Get your parents to help you sort out the easy questions, and then don't hesitate to go back to them with the harder ones that come up later. There will be many, I guarantee you.

One of the *first* lessons parents must teach children is that the world is a spiritually dangerous place, with good and evil, and consequences for each. One of the *dominant* lessons they must teach is that the well-educated adult both thinks and acts righteously at all times, discharging his duties as a subject of our sovereign God. Armed with truth, character, and under God's protection, no Christian is to hide from the dangers but to confront and even expose them. R.C. Sproul, Jr. states, "Our goal is not to raise highbrow pagans but soldiers who not only know their enemies, but know where their weaknesses and strengths lie."[12]

The goal in all Kingdom-related work is the Christianizing of culture by the discipleship process. People who humbly Christianize anti-Christian cultures must inevitably traffic in anti-Christian ideas. But they don't fellowship with those ideas; they reprove them and replace them.[13]

Here's my answer: I believe film is a legitimate tool for this exposing and reproving process. Film certainly is, currently as well as historically, the most powerful and widespread tool for enculturating entire populations. I personally believe Jesus Christ has moral and professional jurisdiction over this industry as well as every other one.

DANCING SHADOWS ON THE SCREEN

Many responsible theologians criticize Christian involvement in any kind of fantasy, as you will quickly

---

12. R.C. Sproul, Jr., "Who's Afraid of the Big Bad Book?" (2001-2002 Veritas Press Catalogue), p. 62.

13. "And do not participate in the unfruitful deeds of darkness, but instead even expose them" (Ephesians 5:11).

discover. (As I've said, difficult questions like these demand intelligent attention. Don't embrace an opinion just because it is in print. Check scripture, and remember to lean on your parents' opinions more than mine. As soon as you find answers for one question, new questions will unfold. Learn to arrive at convictions before you go too far in your plans or you may have a crisis of conscience at a most inopportune time during your career.)

According to Webster's 1828 dictionary, the root meaning of "fantasy" suggests the causing to appear at pleasure, or shooting forth. This is what filmmakers do, even when they bring documentaries to the screen. The image projected on the screen (the organization of the ideas, sounds and impressions) is "fantasy," something the filmmaker caused to appear from his own imagination and design. This he does when producing biographies, comedies, war movies, westerns, documentaries, thrillers and magical fantasies.

The Fantasy genre is easier to classify, since it depicts a type of story that takes the audience to new places where events cannot occur in real life - they transcend the bounds of human possibility and physical laws. Generally, they feature netherworlds filled with magical things that are obviously a departure from reality.

Now consider a different kind of "fantasy" film. Most "realistic" Hollywood productions take place in a fantastic, super-stereotypical world developed by the writers, producers, and directors. In this imaginary world the cops are bigots, the military is stupid, the CIA is evil, all vehicles explode when crashed, all dogs are invincible, all Christians are nutcases, all Buddhists are supernaturally wise, all Muslims are peaceful, all businessmen are corrupt, all fathers are stupid, and sin never has any consequences because there is no sovereign God. This version of reality is every bit as fantastic and untruthful as one that features talking animals or magic unicorns, and is far more harmful.

If fantasy theologies are set in real-world, modern day settings, they can be incredibly destructive. These are not clear-cut Fantasy genre films at all, but typically take place in the present-day world, inserting fantastic themes, paranormal horror or mystical science-fiction ideas. It takes a lot of discernment to explain the subtle error or defiling ideas in such films. They can confuse children and adults even when wise commentary is available. Steven Spielberg's *Close Encounters of the Third Kind* was surrealistically confusing: a few real and especially sensitive Americans encountered real aliens. The concept of real aliens was exotic in the 1970s, but no longer. Surreal films have led the grand deception that real aliens are out there in real life.

But what if we tried to have realistically supernatural characters or circumstances manipulating a real world? What about so-called Christian fantasy like the apocalyptic *Left Behind* movies or Frank Peretti's books, which break the rule, insisting that fantasy elements are actual truth? They didn't work; meaning, they weren't helpful in communicating truth because there was so much confusing error in the theology and speculation in the fantasy.

Frank Peretti's fictionalized accounts of spiritual warfare require him to create an entire hierarchy of heavenly and demonic influence that is not supported by scripture. He places words into the mouths of God and His angels. The story itself might have been more biblically grounded than *It's a Wonderful Life*, but by falsely branding it as an accurate depiction of spiritual truth it does far more damage, and ultimately contains a weaker, less concentrated message.

So does the *Left Behind* series. By dramatizing a Biblically unsound eschatology, the authors have lent credence to a mindset that our task as Christians is simply to wait for God to pull us off the battlefield before the shooting starts. More disturbingly, when the fictional God of this fantasy does this in the film adaptation, the world scarcely notices that the believers are gone, and society suffers little by the absence of Christians. These books, and to a greater extent the resulting movies, faithfully and dramatically represent a misguided tenet of American evangelicalism: Christianity is socially irrelevant, and that's the way it's supposed to be.

As you study the different genres, you can expect to find theological shortcomings in any film, but films that are marketed as being spiritually or theologically accurate must be above reproach in the stories they tell. This is usually not the case, especially in the Historical Drama category.

Because of the dramatic license required to turn a true story into a compelling film, this genre is particularly hard to protect from confusing error. In the hands of a historical revisionist, this can become one of the most precarious genres of all, because all films are fantasies.

A case in point is the *Little House on the Prairie* television series. It is seriously flawed and violates of the Third and Ninth Commandments by misrepresenting God's sovereign authority and falsely recreating the history of an actual family in the 1870s. NBC producers structured it as a series about a 1970s family with a corrupted 1970s worldview wearing 1870s costumes in an 1870s setting. NBC based the series on the true biographical account of a real 1870s family whom God providentially taught, sanctified, honored, blessed and preserved. The truth of God's sovereign work has been denied, perverted, nullified and erased by re-scripting real truth into two-dimensional falsehood.

The theological and historical errors in this re-scripting process were perhaps unintentional, but if young viewers don't understand the difference between the worldviews of the fictional TV Ingalls family and the real, historical Ingalls family, they will be confused and defiled by inexcusable historical revisionism. Does this mean the series shouldn't be viewed by Christians? It's my opinion that Christians shouldn't sit and be entertained by this series, but that it can very helpful to sit and study it. Especially if the Christian viewer intends to be a filmmaker.

Any flawed program is dangerous if the flaws are not pointed out. And every film will have flaws of some sort. This is one of the dangers of the medium, which must be recognized and subdued to the best of the filmmaker's ability. There is fantasy in every production which must be scrupulously controlled by the filmmaker and, more importantly, recognized by the viewer.

I think there are many lessons young viewers can learn from *Little House*, but only if the distortions are exposed and the truth is explained. Film students need to be exposed to error of this kind, preferably by parents who can spot and censure the errors. Christians needn't create superstitious or Pharisaical rules when it comes to issues of fiction. We must recognize any threats of defilement but then take them head-on, subduing any corrupt institutions in Christ's name and with His truth.

Another example of fantastic re-interpretation of historical fact would be the 1997 film *Titanic*. James Cameron spent most of his $200,000,000 budget making sure that his representation of the doomed ship was completely and utterly accurate. He built his sets from the original blueprints, commissioned new carpets and fittings from companies that had originally supplied the White Star Line, and had designers create fabulous costumes that would actually have been in fashion during the 1910s.

However, despite the hours of training in proper 1912 mannerisms, bearing, and posture, the actors who wore these

costumes were denizens of the 1990s. The script was filled
with language, behavior, and ideas that would have been
utterly shocking to men and women living at the turn of the
century, and James Cameron even rewrote the recorded lines
and actions of actual historical figures to better fit them into
his fictional story.

And when the boat finally begins to sink, these modern
extras react in a choreographed humanistic panic. The
orderly and dignified self-sacrifice of the real-life Titanic
passengers is replaced by every-man-for-himself anarchy on
the set. The ship's heroic officers become the film's barbaric
maniacs. The millionaires who died lifting washerwomen
into lifeboats are acted as whining cowards, pleading for
safety and locking the decent poor people behind iron gates
(which the real RMS Titanic did not even have).

The important lessons of a monumental catastrophe
are buried under a Marxist message of class-warfare, and
the demonstration of the universally-accepted Christian
duty of "women and children first" was erased by clever
screenwriting. A historical event that illustrated the largely
Christian ethic of pre-modern world was forgotten because
the 1997 movie was set not in real life history, but within
the modern worldview created by Cameron's personal
religious presuppositions.

And because such a great effort was taken to make the
film look as realistic as possible, and no expense was spared
in replicating certain visual realities, the fantastic elements

are all the more convincing. This fantasy film slanders the heroism of Christian men and denies the true actions of a largely Christian society.

Today's film culture is habitually anti-Christian, but that custom can be subdued and changed by building a better film culture outside of Hollywood. The grammar of film is predominantly fantasy, but that too can be brought under the disciplines of the faith.

Many Christians realize this, and tend to place an undeserved amount of praise on JRR Tolkien for creating a powerful allegory of the Christian faith; almost deifying his goals, his books, and the resulting films. This is a very dangerous position to take; unqualified endorsement of media can be just as destructive as unqualified condemnation. Tolkien was a Catholic professor of ancient languages, and not a sterling example of Christianity. His goal in writing *Lord of the Rings* was merely to create for England the same sort of epic mythology found in other early European cultures. However, his strengths as writer and storyteller are unmatched, largely because of his understanding of Christian narrative that he added to his pagan myth.

But before any particular genre can be truly redeemed by truth, the filmmaker needs to know the strength and weakness of every literary and cinematic device for every genre. These include recognizable patterns, syntax, filmic techniques or conventions: settings (and props), content and subject matter, themes, period, plot, central narrative events, motifs, styles, structures, situations, recurring icons, stock characters (or characterizations). The filmmaker must apply his solutions imaginatively and figuratively. A first step is in the study of biblical literary devices. A good second step is in studying every film literary device, including the figurative language of the culture of the filmgoer.

What I have concluded in my study is that fantasy is an acceptable device for teaching lessons that need to be taught to an audience that is familiar with the structure of fantasy. Show-biz is supposed to contain elements of wonder, awe and the extraordinary. Every film of every genre is fantastical. Some genres are more easily redeemable than others, and some are dangerous in the hands of any filmmaker, but all films are fantasies, and if this troubles you, you're getting into the wrong business.

THE RESPONSIBILITIES OF TEACHING

Once you're "in pictures," you are a teacher. Even if you start out at the bottom of the industry ladder, you are an accomplice to every message in every film to which you contribute your talents and abilities. As you go through this book, a series of questions will continue to be asked of you. Whose side are you on? Are you disciplined enough to produce your own life first and then media projects later? Do you have an honest worldview that's rooted in the truth? What stories do you have to tell that are worth telling? These are important questions. If you have nothing to teach, you don't want to get into a vocation that teaches.

But if you do have something to say, what kinds of films will you make? Because this book emphasizes the necessity of spiritual maturity, some readers may jump to the conclusion that I believe the only good films would be super-spiritual sorts of Christian propaganda, with gospel presentations, scenes from evangelistic meetings, sinners' prayers, saints' prayers, pietistic heroes and Christian symbols, churches, hymns, and other religious imagery—followed by an altar call. Not so. My theology informs me that I don't have to "sell" the truth.[14] I just have to tell it well and with integrity.

And that truth is not limited to the "four spiritual laws." The Bible makes it clear that we are to make disciples of nations, "teaching all things whatsoever I have commanded." This means that every potential subject discussed in Scripture is grounds for teaching and for storytelling. This means that I can honor Christ by making biblical films about the meaning of play, about family life, about the animal kingdom, about relationships, or anything which rightly falls within the domain of a Christian worldview.

Are the only acceptable movies "G" or "PG" rated ones? Not necessarily, though they be the most profitable. Can evil and vice appear in a film? They certainly appear in the Bible. The issue comes down to what you intend to teach about evil and vice and how you plan to portray them. If evil is

---

14. Romans 9; Ephesians 1:4,5; Isaiah 43:12; Acts 13:48; Matthew 22:14; Romans 8:29.

artfully portrayed and presented as evil, it will discourage, not incite others to imitate it. In fact, a key ingredient of righteous storytelling is the redemption of evildoers.

When I was seven years old, I remember having a discussion with a neighbor's son about Captain Haddock in the *Tintin* comics. My friend's mother wouldn't allow him to read the *Tintin* books because someone drank whiskey in the story. I think I knew then what a thorough lesson was taught by that fictional whiskey bottle about the nature of drunkenness and how it turned Tintin's friend from an ally into a terrible nemesis. All I ever needed to know about intemperance I learned vividly and accurately from a fictional gentleman named Tintin.

Every story and every scene in every film teaches something. Every film teaches the director's version of truth. Most movies today are so loaded with confused versions of half-truth, even the director doesn't know the extent of the error and propaganda he's putting into the market.

As this book will show, even many Christian filmmakers can't recognize the amount of error and exploitation they pack into their own scripts. Thus their films can tend to propagandize viewers in ways the filmmakers never would have intended.[15] Good filmmakers recognize propaganda

---

15. See James 3:1. You can't afford to be a literary novice or a biblical illiterate in this business, because God will hold you accountable for every project you put your hand to do, and every word in every script you write, produce, or direct. You will face greater scrutiny and stricter judgment from God as a teacher—a teacher of theology and morality.

because they are wise, and then they excise it from the film because they know they don't need it to teach the true lessons that naturally come through their films.

Good filmmakers are not afraid to let their films teach what is true. My idea of a good movie is one that is *error-free*, not in the sense that we never see error, but that the movie explains error truthfully in a Christ-honoring way. Thus a movie's brief story may touch on the hideous, the fiendish, or the dreadful, so long as the viewer is not defiled in the process through a gratuitous presentation of wickedness, and such wicked manifestations are resolved and explained in light of God's standards.

A good film is simply a representation of life from a truthful point of view. Simply capturing the truth in a story and playing it out on screen will teach many lessons that are rarely seen or heard in the media of the post-Christian West. This is how it is possible for evil to legitimately appear, briefly, in a film. Evil cannot be exploited but must be accurately exposed. It must not be glamorized but carefully portrayed. It must not be allowed to prosper, but ultimately fail, as it does both stage-front and behind-the-scenes as God unfolds covenantal history. Your stories can take a viewer behind the scenes of real life to see truth at its most dramatic and personal.

The essence of drama lies in the way people face everyday moral challenges or conflicts. Villains usually fail those tests and suffer the consequences. Heroes struggle to pass those tests and reap the benefits of their victories, whether big victories or small ones. A good movie can tell anyone's story in any setting. A good movie will have moral drama. Moral jeopardy. Moral tension. Moral conflict. And most importantly of all, moral elucidation. A good movie will always have enough moral clarity that the audience will know who the good guys are and who the bad guys are, and why there is a difference. Ditto for good ideas and bad ideas. In a good movie, the protagonist is brought within range of personal redemption. A string of good movies will contribute to healthy moral discernment in viewers, building loyalties for virtues and aversion to vices. This string of movies will not be made inside Hollywood.

Today's Christian filmmakers need to realize they have grown up in an apostate culture—one that dulls the senses. It's not easy to discern those things that make for good cinema and dangerous cinema. Spiritual maturity is the road to discernment and the road to success as a heroic filmmaker.

If you will submit yourself to God's word, wise counsel and firmly discipline yourself against compromise, then you may have what it takes to be an independent Christian filmmaker. If you can humbly bring yourself to the point where you can triumph over the dangers of the industry and become a champion of what is true, then may God bless you. You're on the right course. You are on track to summoning the determination to be a teacher—the right kind of teacher. But you must never think you've arrived at any kind of professional apogee. For your entire life and career, you should surround yourself with advisers and colleagues who are wiser than you are. This book contains some good advice from some wise men. Add that advice to what your godly parents have taught you. If you then decide to build a vocation as a filmmaker, then may God doubly bless you as you attain the double honor that goes with the hard work of teaching.

Chapter 2

THINKING LIKE A WARRIOR

Storytelling is the most powerful way to put ideas into the world today. —*Robert McKee*

The power of the up-and-coming independent Christian film movement is found not merely in it message, but its methodology. Perhaps the most significant tool available to those working outside Hollywood is the influence for good found in godly mentoring. The same spirit of creativity and mentorship that has grown the American Christian home school movement to nearly five million, is birthing a new generation of independent filmmakers. My own testimony is that of a son who was lovingly nurtured and discipled as a filmmaker by my father. The sacrificial and visionary spirit of my father as a mentor has shaped and defined my worldview, directed my steps, protected me from harm, and opened for me remarkable doors of opportunity.

I was born into a media-saturated world that was largely a media-controlled world. Because my father produced a daily national television program, some of the first words I learned were about the business of production. I didn't know what it all meant, but whatever it was that Dad was doing when he was "on a shoot" sounded fun and important. I wanted in on it.

Fortunately, my dad didn't keep me in the dark or at arm's length. He pulled me in close to himself and gave me a figurative flashlight I could use to peer into the dark corners of a mysterious industry. He told me about my world and my times, and he carefully showed it to me—warts and all. He wanted me to know about the potent influence of media and what it was doing to the people around us. And he told me a lot about Hollywood—that small, morally confounded city which manipulates virtually every cultural trend I will battle for the rest of my life.

These interesting lessons began to carry a message my father never let me forget. In light of reality, particularly spiritual reality, life is a *battleground*. Because filmmaking is such a fun profession, young media people can make the serious blunder of viewing life as *playground*. My dad never wanted me to make that mistake.

This may be the reason he had me cut my teeth on political media before I ever touched entertainment media. Political media has the unmistakable smell of battle. Mao once said that politics is war without bloodshed and that war is politics with bloodshed. He also said that political power comes out of the barrel of a gun. Many of his disciples discovered that even more political power comes out of the lens of a movie projector.

Political media defines the battleground we're camped on. Entertainment media illustrates the theology of our culture. By giving me an education in politics and theology, my dad prepared me to handle the dangerous weapon called media or, rather, to at least get close enough to filmmaking to study it rationally.

THE MEDIA OF MY GENERATION

Films interested my father, and they fascinated me. Because I was taught to analyze films, I never really found them to be very glamorous or even emotionally immersive. Because I was taught to search for the hidden worldview in a film, I tended to look at film content the way Sovietologists of the time deciphered cryptic messages from the Kremlin. It was a good academic exercise, and unraveling the technical side of the industry was even more enjoyable.

The technology within a film is actually not that complex. Even neophyte filmmakers can set up a few lights, position a few actors, shoot some film, cut it together, and tell a story that makes an audience laugh or cry or imitate what they've just seen. Books make people think. Films make people feel, and feelings are what make people think, and then think again, and keep thinking. With just a few feet of film, one can change the worldview of millions of people. And that's what filmmakers have been doing at a sophisticated level.

The industry is not a dream industry, it is a teaching industry. Many of the teachers involved in filmmaking are dedicated mercenaries, political extremists, artistic militants, and cultural activists. These teachers know the film industry is no storybook world. They are fully aware that it is a real-life battleground, and they do battle accordingly.

I was too young to remember the first movie set I visited, but Dad took me along anyway, as part of an upbringing that has ever since been a fascinating orientation to the dominant teaching institution of my time. When I was two years old, the world's most influential film director was Francis Ford Coppola. Dad had received clearance from him to observe, over a period of weeks, a closed location in Oklahoma where Coppola was making two films back-to-back.[16]

I think I might vaguely remember the catering truck. If I had been older, I'm sure I would have noticed and remembered many more important things. Coppola was utilizing some experimental editing technology on that shoot that would have fascinated me. He had a video editing station right on the set with him. He recorded video straight from the viewfinder on the film camera and sent it to the

---

16. Coppola had purchased the rights to author S.E. Hinton's novels *The Outsiders* and *Rumble Fish* and was targeting the teen market with the release of two separate films. Zoetrope Studios produced; Warner Brothers distributed.

edit room (a motor home). After each scene, he would review the tape, cut it to the preceding scene, and see if it worked before he set up the next sequence. It's a lot of work to set up and take down sequences, especially when one works with perfectionist production designers like Coppola's favorite, Dean Tavoularis. Coppola's technology was a creative solution to an age-old film problem, and Coppola was breaking it in.

He was also breaking-in some new acting talent. Coppola had pulled in Tom Cruise, Matt Dillon, Ralph Macchio, Patrick Swayze, Rob Lowe, Emilio Estevez, Diane Lane, Tom Waits, Laurence Fishburne, Mickey Rourke, Vince Spano, Nicolas Cage, and other little-known names. Coppola's daughter Sophia was eleven at the time, and spent many afternoons perched on her father's knee, watching and learning.

LEARNING ABOUT BASIC PRIORITIES

Over the next few years, I did the same with my father. When I was four, my father had an opportunity to go to Los Angeles and work as a filmmaker in the entertainment capital of the world. Instead, he moved his family in the opposite direction, for priorities that were bigger than success, money, glamour, resume, or even personal preference. It was a good decision.

That was how I found myself in Washington, D.C., where my dad founded a production company focused on political media. He started with a small studio in our home.

Fortunately, my parents had decided to home school my siblings and me, so I was home all the time, and could watch everything that went on. I watched my father choosing projects and literally picking battles, for reasons of priority.

This was perhaps the most important thing I learned about filmmaking. The first opportunity, the first idea, the first option may not be the right one. Thinking twice and thinking wisely must be the precedent to any media decision. Because you live in a media-dominated world, your first instinct may be off-base. Think twice. Then get counsel from your families and the Word of God. Then think twice again.

LEARNING ABOUT BASIC FILMMAKING

When I was twelve years old, I worked as a grip, carrying and setting up gear. When I was thirteen, I could say "we" were making long-form documentaries, promotional materials for political candidates, television commercials, and media for think tanks. By the time I was sixteen, I had worked in almost every aspect of television production, even animation. I liked it all. I liked the challenge of computer-generated animation the best. This is probably because, as an animator, I was a real filmmaker. For my animations, I was writer, director, director of photography, gaffer, dolly grip, stunt coordinator, costume designer, and production designer. Animation involves setting up every shot from scratch. Every element has to be created. Every hand-created actor must be manipulated into every action, right down to individual eye blinks. Animation teaches about making shots work, making scenes work, and about directing every element of every scene.

Three-dimensional animated films, such as the kind made by Pixar (*Toy Story*, *Finding Nemo*), must be created from nothing but ideas. There are no physical props, cameras, or lights, and therefore no physical limits. I loved 3D animation because it was teaching me about the fundamentals of filmmaking. I needed to be fluent in the "grammar" of filmmaking before I could tell the computer where to put a prop, a light, or a camera. I had to know about editing in order to know how long to make a scene. I had to learn about everything, or my 3D animations looked empty and incomplete.

So I studied the great directors, the pictorial storytellers. Kurosawa, John Ford, Ridley Scott, Steven Spielberg, and I looked for the small details about how they moved their cameras, their actors, their landscapes, and their lights. I studied their cuts. I read their scripts. I was looking for the grammar of filmmaking. It is a largely visual language that must be mastered in order to communicate a coherent, meaningful visual story. The grammar of filmmaking changes over time, in the same way that the grammar of Shakespeare is different from the grammar of *TIME* magazine. Same language, but a slightly different syntax is used to create similar meaning.

Filmmakers all over the world have learned essentially the same grammar for the language of filmmaking. Some nationalities may develop some elements to a more advanced state. Jackie Chan, for example, gradually increased the speed of his fight-scene elements until they were far more sophisticated than the stunt fighting choreographed in Hollywood and far more coherent than the earlier Bruce Lee films. Jackie utilized the same grammar of the Hollywood slug fest, but invented a faster "dialect" with some new verbs.

I realized I needed to learn the grammar of filmmaking before I could create meaningful productions. When I was eighteen, I moved with my family to New Zealand, just months after New Line Cinema's historic decision to hire Peter Jackson to direct *The Lord of the Rings*. Through my dad's connections, I obtained an opportunity to help launch New Zealand's first 3D animated television show, a children's series. Our final product looked far more expensive than our competitors', and attracted plenty of interest from overseas producers. Our second show was a co-production with Weta Workshop, *Lord of the Rings*' famous and suddenly Oscar-laden effects house.

At age twenty-one, I had not reached my goal of becoming a director, but I found myself at a vocational pinnacle where I could relate professionally with peers who were at the very top of their game, at the very top of the industry. Animation provided me a great vantage point. I enjoyed meetings with the guys who cooked up the breakthroughs I wanted to know about—the technicians who created the life in *Monsters, Inc.,* the artists who made World War II so real in *Band of Brothers,* and many of the very clever and resourceful people at Weta Digital. These were the fellows who spoke a fascinating new dialect in the language of filmmaking. These other young pros were both imagining and pursuing a new vision for the industry. They were driving this vision from deep behind the scenes.

Up to that point in life, I had been studying filmmaking's past. Now I am in a position to watch the charting of filmmaking's future. The opportunities that open up at times like these are attractive, tempting, and exhilarating. Working with the most fascinating technology of our time in the most colorful industry of our time is stimulating and dizzyingly fun. Under these conditions, finding one's way through a maze of decisions about one's life and career is not easy. My twenty-first year was one of complex decision-making.

How does the aspiring media professional discern the difference between exciting opportunities and wise opportunities? What are the answers to tough questions about culture, vocation, stewardship, and personal income? Decisions must be made for reasons of priority, with wisdom.

ONE LARGELY UNUSED SECRET WEAPON IN DECISION-MAKING

Today's dysfunctional generation has lost touch with a powerfully traditional concept of family. I expect that many readers of this book have been brought up with a modern outlook on family and career. Some of you don't think of yourselves as a vital part of a broadly multigenerational family. You see yourselves as individuals with mere sentimental attachments to family—free agents whose decisions don't much affect your family.

I personally believe family attachments can and must be stronger than sentiment, especially for those of you looking at a vocation in media. Any direct or indirect advice offered in this book is built on the idea that parental counsel can be invaluable, and that the structure of one's family or family-centered lifestyle should never be compromised because of job opportunities. If we media people are creative enough to work in a creative industry, we can use that creativity to devise, build and maintain lifestyles that take full advantage of multigenerational family strengths. The wisest filmmakers of the next generation will be ones who heeded elders, even elders who knew nothing about the film's arts or sciences. Listen carefully and think twice before you proceed.

Chapter 3

TRAINING AND QUALIFICATIONS

*And the Lord spake unto Moses, saying, See, I have
called by name Bezaleel. And I have filled him with the
spirit of God, in wisdom, and in understanding, and
in knowledge, and in all manner of workmanship, To
devise cunning works.... And I, behold, I have given
with him Aholiab, and in the hearts of all that are wise
hearted I have put wisdom, that they may make all that
I have commanded thee.   —Exodus 31:1-6*

Because my dad started to teach me about media before
I could talk, I grew up listening. Sometimes more
carefully than other times, but much of what I know was
simply handed to me by a man who knew what he was
talking about professionally. I'm grateful for this. It saved me
years of learning the hard way; receiving scars from my own
weapons and getting clobbered by people I thought were
my allies.

What about aspiring filmmakers whose parents don't know media? Below is a summary of the most important things I learned about being a learner, and about being in a family, and about breaking into the industry. No matter who you may be, your parents know more about media than you think they know, primarily because media is religious communication. Forays into its realm need religious wisdom and the plain common sense that comes from maturity.

Making films can be as noble as any other profession and is an entirely legitimate pursuit for Christians. This is not because filmmaking is something special. It is because of the inherent dignity in all dominion-oriented work. In fact, when filmmaking is compared with other pursuits, it has little to commend it to a responsible adult as a high-class vocation. Walter Matthau once observed that films are made by morons for morons.[17] A stroll through any video store corroborates and illustrates this observation.

Many filmmakers have legitimate regrets about the films they have made and about the lives they have led. This is primarily because they were followers and not leaders. The only thing that can make this tarnished vocation noble is the nobility of the content and the integrity of the filmmaker. Unless a filmmaker brings these two virtues into the industry, he will be subsumed by the persistent seediness of a squalid and nasty business. There is one other thing that

---

17. Quoted by Lloyd Billingsley in *The Seductive Image* (Wheaton: Crossway Books, 1989), p. 61.

will serve the young filmmaker well: a vision to teach what is true. Visionaries never lose sight of this potential. Lenin knew there was more to film than moronic entertainment. "Communists must always consider that of all the arts the motion picture is the most important," he said.[18]

Immature media people, including immature Christians, produce dangerous media, and will themselves be damaged by the wrong associations with corrupt media "professionals." Parental input is a practical remedy for immaturity. Parents do not need to be film experts to build maturity into their young film students. All wisdom is helpful.

If a student stumbles into the industry without having had some parental guidance and parental blessing, he is very likely to become a total disciple of the industry, adopting and perpetuating its errors—especially its theological errors. Parents, it is your duty to supervise and disciple the film student from a young age. Parents must provide ongoing input and opinions about everything the student needs to learn and what he thinks he needs to learn.

This has nothing to do with the technical details, but it has *everything* to do with the ideals portrayed in the stories being told. Parents and pastors need to actively explain the messages in the media studied, especially the movies. If they

---

18. K.L. Billingsley, *Hollywood Party: How Communism Seduced the American Film Industry in the 1930s and 1940s* (California: Prima Publishing, 1998), p. 20.

can't explain the subtleties of a specific dangerous worldview, a student should not be exposed to that particular film, television show, commercial, news program, video game, or book, no matter what technical or artistic merits it might have.

This is important because all filmmakers are tellers of moral, or immoral, stories. Sound morality comes from years of training one's senses to discern good and evil. The foundation for this discernment is built best in the home, around the family hearth, the family Bible, the family church, and, occasionally, the family television screen. Candid family discussions about the Bible and the media can go a long way to give a future media mogul a solid, morally correct worldview.

The film industry is the most complex of interdisciplinary industries. Art, music, science, business, information technology, history, and theology cannot be separated from each other in the making of a motion picture. To learn how all these disciplines work together takes a lot of study. Studying industry movies requires looking very closely at some of them… spending time with them… spending time with the ideas and messages in them.

Students of film tend to be attentive learners, because they must teach themselves to be observant and receptive in order to learn their craft. However, if they are more receptive to Hollywood's messages than to parental messages,[19] they will fail even as craftsmen. The will learn only to craft harmful messages.

It was the Puritan writer Richard Baxter who identified the truth that vocations that harm the soul will eventually "wrong the souls" of others. "Choose that employment or calling in which you may be most serviceable to God," Baxter wrote. "Choose not that in which you may be most rich or honorable in the world; but that in which you may do most good, and best escape sinning."[20]

In short, the student should bail out of media if he can't work in it without sinning, because without a pure heart, the student can't learn what is necessary about the correct worldview. Even the technical aspects of film are completely enmeshed in its theology, history, political science, ethics, and law.

Today it is often the worst films ideologically that are the best films technically, and to glean the technical knowledge from these films will require sitting through a barrage of bad ideas. Obviously, it takes spiritual maturity to survive, or even to know which educational influences to subject oneself

---

19. The student must heed the voice of his parents. The student is not really listening to his parents unless he has willingly and obediently given them his heart. This is a biblical concept. It's a command to every son or daughter. In the most simplistic of terms, this means the student is actively and genuinely interested in what his parents know, what they think, and what they want.

20. Yvonne S. Smith, "The Myths of Good Hard Work: Vocation and Destiny in the 21st Century." Paper delivered at Biola University in March 2002.

to. And every media vocation is a religious vocation because it is educational. All education is religious. Every media project teaches religious ideas.

The reason this is true is simple. Education proceeds along the lines of a worldview, which dictates presuppositions about God, man, time, justice, civilization, and the very meaning of life. These are all inescapably religious ideas with very definite theological truth. The *Star Wars* films are built on a particular theology. So is *Seinfeld*, *ER*, and the evening news.

CHARACTER QUALIFICATIONS

The following questions can help both parent and student, especially as you think of these as primary qualifications for succeeding in the industry.

Are you living in the real world?

Many film students immerse themselves so deeply into flawed industries that create only fictional worlds that they lose touch with reality. The film student needs to be able to see his frailties, his fears, and his weaknesses with clarity at all times, that he may deal with them humbly and penitently.

Are you a leader or a follower?

An exposure to the world of relativistic fiction can conform students to the shallow dream worlds created by Hollywood. Strong Christians must be willing and able to stand above it and lead viewers away from the comfortable and familiar. Of course, with his parents and other mentors, he must be a ready disciple, but with others he must become a fearless disciple-maker.

Are you weak in faith, or strong?

It takes a burning desire and profound confidence to rely on God's strength to challenge the industry. Too many students would rather join the ranks of industry professionals as "one of them," never rocking the boat.

Are you teaching with truth and sound doctrine?

Filmmakers are people with something to say. They are storytellers. This is precisely why they must have the maturity to say the right things. Mature students will not be waiting for their movies to premiere before they present their messages. They will be doing it with friends, peers, associates, and strangers on a small scale. They will be studying their doctrine now so that they are certain they are on the right track. They will be filling their minds with what is good, right, noble, and excellent.[21] The prolific western novelist Louis L'Amour once said a writer's brain is like a magician's hat. Something must be put into it before anything can come out.

Are you growing in grace and humility?

The development of character is proof that growth is taking place. The virtues of grace, humility, and temperance

---

21. Philippians 4:8, "Finally, brethren, whatsoever things are true, whatsoever things are honest, whatsoever things are just, whatsoever things are pure, whatsoever things are lovely, whatsoever things are of good report; if there be any virtue, and if there be any praise, think on these things."

are foundational for men who would be teachers. Even in Hollywood's twisted ideals of business, it is obvious that men without grace and humility make lousy directors. Once they get reputations as jerks, the true professionals won't work with them. A question often asked about a director is, "is he a headset-smasher?" This is the jargon to describe a short-tempered director who handles the frustrations of the job with tantrum-like antics with his headphones. No one wants to work with a headset-smasher because of the smasher's character shortcomings. He will tend to deal with every issue—from money to the feelings of staff—with the same explosive, disrespectful impulses.

Do you have vigor and spiritual authority?

Men with good messages carry a force of personality that reflects the weight and sobriety of their message, life purpose, and personal character.

Are you pursuing a relationship with God through biblical literacy?

Too many proud filmmakers are content with a spirituality that is based on nothing but feelings, misplaced pride, vain imagination, and self will. A student will never know God's mind or His will without continual reference to the Word of God.

Are you building your own convictions?

Most young filmmakers are too content to coast along on the convictions of others. Without your own convictions, you will not be able to discern good from evil.

If the answer to even a few of these questions is "no," you are not qualified to step out onto the battlefield. You are either not ready but will be in the future, or you are chasing a film career for the wrong motives. Either way, parents and students must refocus preparation on the building of personal character or the young filmmaker could become an accomplice to an outlaw occupation.

They must understand the traditions of men and why they are dangerous. They must be constantly perfecting a dynamic biblical worldview that will guide projects and decisions. They must have messages they desperately want the world to know. This is just a crash course in some important basics of some very complicated issues of maturity, wisdom, and spiritual leadership.

ACADEMIC QUALIFICATIONS

When I visit television and film schools, I come away feeling sorry for the students. They are not being taught very much that is helpful, and most of them are depressed because they know this. The mood in these facilities reminds me of John T. Gatto's gloomy description of today's school experience and what it produces: "physical, moral, and intellectual paralysis."[22]

---

22. See John Taylor Gatto, *An Underground History of American Education* (New York: Oxford Village Press, 2001).

Today's media students are working with equipment and software that will be obsolete before they finish school. Some, if not all, of their teachers are people who can't make it in the industry, and the environment is bleak because many classmates enroll simply to kill time. They don't know *what* they want to be when they grow up. With the exception of large schools like UCLA,[23] few grads find employment solely using their academic credentials.

With some employers, credentials are a hindrance because the degree says, "the holder of these credentials just spent four years in a dismally unproductive environment using gear that is no longer industry standard, trying to succeed in a totally artificial environment because he didn't have the resourcefulness or creativity to go out and produce something for the real world." Employers in media organizations want to know only one thing: is this applicant "switched-on?" Switched-on employees are simultaneously *resourceful, talented, capable, dependable, accomplished, entrepreneurial, and honest.* Most eager writers/producers/directors are so switched-on, they're too busy to be bogged down in an artificial environment with people who are

---

23. UCLA is known in the film industry as "Hollywood's employment agency." The industry tends to look at UCLA film students and grads as a ready pool of part-time manpower, not so much because it is a superior school, but because it is geographically convenient and attracts teachers who are still attached to the industry. If a student intends to succeed in filmmaking by going the Hollywood route, by starting at the bottom of a corrupt system, UCLA may be an academic experience that would open doors and make contacts. However, this route is not recommended.

not motivated. They simply start teaching themselves the things they need to know to produce, and then they begin producing. I doubt that the execs at New Line Cinema inquired into the academic qualifications of Peter Jackson before they entrusted him with several hundred million dollars. They were more interested in his abilities and record of accomplishment. From a young age, Jackson was too busy making films to go to film school. And it's the same scenario for the best filmmakers worldwide.

My father has had to evaluate hundreds of potential media employees. I've watched him bypass many with sterling academic resumes and bring on the guys with the real portfolios: excerpts of projects they created on their own. I've personally evaluated applications of hundreds of animators from all over the world. The academic credential is the last thing I look at. The best animators I've ever worked with have been self-taught, and so were the entrepreneurs who built the film industry.

Chapter 4

HOW HOLLYWOOD CREATED ITSELF

Hollywood is engaged in the mass production
of prefabricated daydreams. It tries to adapt the
American dream, that all men are created equal, to
the view that all men's dreams should be made equal.
—*Hortense Powdermaker*[24]

The creation of modern motion picture technology began in 1888, when George Eastman developed the Kodak camera, which used rolls of his paper negative film. This flexible film was far easier to manipulate within the camera than the glass plates used previously. The paper film was soon replaced with celluloid, and George Muybridge of England used a number of these cameras to take a series of photographs of a running horse.

---

24. Hortense Powdermaker, *Hollywood the Dream Factory: An Anthropologist Looks at the Movie Makers* (Boston: Little, Brown, 1950), p. 39.

The new film, and this experiment, which served to settle a bet about whether all four hooves were off the ground at a time, came to the attention of Thomas Edison. He and an assistant developed their own camera, the Kinetograph, which took advantage of the flexible celluloid by running it over sprockets through the camera in a short loop. Short filmed sequences could then be shown in coin-operated cabinets called Kinetoscopes. Kinetoscope arcades popped up much like the video-game arcades of the 1980s. But only one person at a time could view the short novelty films. It seemed film had little scope as a mass-media phenomenon.

However, two Frenchmen were experimenting with and improving the sprocket and shutter mechanisms of Edison's camera. The Lumière brothers borrowed a few principles from the sewing machines of the day, and built a camera that held the film still to be exposed, and then jerked it forward to the next frame as the shutter cycled, which resulted in better image quality and partly reduced film's flickering effect.

Their camera's new sprocket technology turned out to be equally effective in a projector, making it possible to show films before a large audience. They patented this method as the Cinématographe, and film became a collective experience. The subject matter of the French films were short plays and Vaudeville-type acts. These demonstrated the mass appeal of emotional content, something even silent films could deliver very powerfully. Emotionally-moved audiences wanted to view the filmed stories again and again.

This lesson was not lost on American entrepreneurs. The first decade of the twentieth century saw robust developments of the industry in America. Consistently clement weather and lighter tax laws brought small production companies to California, where they would develop into five dominant studios. The vaudeville films of Mack Sennett pulled together actors and directors such as Carole Lombard, Mary Pickford, Charlie Chaplin, and David Ward Griffith, creating the beginnings of the "star system."

FROM VOYEUR TO PARTICIPANT

In my opinion, D.W. Griffith was the true father of entertainment cinema. Before his early experiments, directors simply used the camera as an extension of the traditional stage, shooting the action of traditional plays from the front, scene by scene, inserting "dialogue slates" that explained what was going on. Inserting the slates was almost the only editing performed. These films were known as "the flickers."

But D.W. Griffith understood that any complex story needed complex visual storytelling aids, and he developed these by simply moving the camera around and having the actors perform accordingly. Then he edited accordingly, which gave him yet new insights into the arts of storytelling. Griffith invented long shots and close-ups, and brought actual depth to film, which allowed the viewer to lose himself in the drama as an intimate participant in the story. Griffith cut his scenes into smaller shots, and edited them together to build pacing, suspense, tension, and emotional moments. Thus, filming and editing techniques came to contribute to the emotional structure of theatrical storytelling. The grammar of filmmaking was becoming more complex, more artistic.

This was the beginning of filmmaking as an art form. The art enhanced the emotional power of the medium, as European political strategists were delighted to discover. Young Soviet propagandist and Red Army veteran Sergei Eisenstein picked up where D.W. Griffith left off, incorporating complex editing techniques to create time and space in a stories that were both epic in scale and intimate in personal involvement. He conducted experiments in framing and editing, and his second feature, *Battleship Potemkin*, remains one of the most politically compelling films ever made.

Back in Hollywood, further changes had occurred with the invention of synchronized sound. Al Jolson's 1927 *The Jazz Singer* showcased the new technology, but despite its success at the box office, many studios looked upon the new technology as merely an expensive gimmick. Alfred Hitchcock made Britain's first "talkie" by shooting some sound sequences of "Blackmail" secretly. His studio bosses agreed to release the final film in both sound and silent versions, as only a few theaters were sound capable at the time.

But sound was more than a just passing fad, and early adopters Fox and Warner Brothers leaped ahead of the more traditionally powerful studios. The huge expense in new, experimental gear for sound recording bankrupted most smaller companies, further cementing the big five into their positions of cultural dominance, further closing the industry to outsiders, beginners, and non-Hollywood players.

Studios which tried to perpetuate the silent era went out of business. With the exception of Charlie Chaplin, slapstick comic actors were scrapped in favor of talent from Vaudeville's new breed—stand-up comedians from New York stages like W.C. Fields, Will Rogers, and Bob Hope. Broadway directors and stars were quickly snapped up in an effort to satisfy the demands of urban moviegoers. It was a magical era. Audiences could see aspects of showbiz they had only read about. The big stars arrived in hometowns on celluloid every Friday, talking and singing and playing music.

Sound changed the very style of film, partly due to the new bulky equipment that was required, but mostly because of the new opportunities that sound afforded. The new Broadway-experienced staff were employed to create a string of popular musicals, both showcasing the new technology and providing new product for entertainment-starved survivors of the Great Depression.

George Cukor and Busby Berkely cranked out a series of films that defined the musical extravaganza genre: glitz, dancing girls, chorus lines, geometric choreography, and bright lights. The novelty of glamour wore thin after so many extravaganzas, but Hollywood was beginning to discover how fast movies could move without pausing for dialogue slates.

A new style of action film, one in which dramatic tension could be created by uninterrupted scenes that built tension to new heights, whetted appetites for yet more tension. Audiences were intrigued by crime stories and gritty, violent gangster films spawned by Warner Brothers, usually starring James Cagney or Edward G. Robinson. Hollywood was now racing into racy content and unprecedented influence with these compelling and convincing new worlds.

However, one of the most powerful influences on Hollywood was the work done by Walt Disney and his team of writers, animators, and technicians. Not only did they invent the art of animation almost from scratch, they developed new storytelling technique with their first films, pioneering the more efficient uses of storyboards, color design, editing styles, music and sound integration and more, that went far beyond anything being done at the time.[25]

Today's live-action blockbusters probably owe more to Disney's first animated features than other films of the same period. Furthermore, Walt's keen business sense

---

25. To read more about this history, I recommend *The Illusion of Life: Disney Animation,* written by Frank Thomas and Ollie Johnston, two of Disney's original Nine Old Men.

and entrepreneurial spirit motivated other studios to stay competitively efficient and productive, and his desire to create wholesome stories for families helped to maintain Hollywood's moral compass for many years.

THE GOLDEN AGE

There have always been strong political and philosophical influences evident in the film industry, as evidenced by the intense social commentaries of early films like the German science fiction film *Metropolis* (1927). Even so, during its early days, Hollywood was more mercenary than ideological. The vast majority of filmgoers were sensible folks with a worldview rich in the moral capital of Christendom. Even unbelieving filmmakers in Hollywood attempted to understand this audience and provide memorable family entertainment. In 1930, the Hays Motion Picture Production Code was put into place, which was a self-imposed ban on sex, violence, and profanity. Modern critics see this adherence to "so-called morality" as the beginning of Hollywood's downfall. Some say that prevented younger, more progressive directors from expressing the full extent of their creative potential, and thus prevented film from being realized as a truthful expression of modern life.

This is untrue. The adherence to Christian ideals and biblical principles of morality encouraged mature, sophisticated, entertaining, and heroic films, which is precisely why modern historians and Hollywood aficionados view this era with contempt. From their perspective, restrictions like the Hays Motion Picture Production Code are a modern incarnation of a puritanical Christianity. Consequently, many film historians are reluctant to see Hollywood's Golden Age for what it really was— entrepreneurial business success—a vigorous industry selling middle America what middle America wanted—innovation, patriotism, action, drama, good versus evil, sophisticated manners, intelligent dialogue, and good-looking lead actors.

German and French cinema, on the other hand, was highly experimental, morally unfettered, and culturally decadent. However, many of the films from this era were most innovative from a professional and artistic standpoint. The best and worst of these was *Triumph of the Will*, a Hitler-sponsored and Nazi-distributed account of the 1934 Nurnburg Rally, beautifully shot and edited by Leni Reifenstahl.

To this day, Refenstahl's work is unchallenged as an example of grand symbolism and disciplined technical achievement (and the power of an unlimited budget). It is one of the most effective pieces of propaganda ever created, largely because it was a perfect combination of art and technique. (Note to young filmmakers: never underestimate the power of solid, professional technique. Once you've learned it, never use it in the service of unworthy projects.)

The visual styles and narrative ideas pioneered in European films trickled into Hollywood during the pre-war period, along with a new influx of actors and directors.

The successes of Hollywood films were very attractive for a number of British professionals, such as Alfred Hitchcock and Laurence Olivier, who relocated to California. As Nazi socialism began to triumph throughout Europe, French and German talent fled to the West as well.[26]

Those who wanted to make movies went to Hollywood. Runaway American teens went to Hollywood seeking fame, fortune, and a piece of the moviemaking vocation. At this point in history, known as the "Golden Age," Hollywood was more productive, popular, and profitable than at any other time. Why did Hollywood have this monopoly power, influence, and draw?

Banking is one reason. The decision-makers with the money were there. The star system is another reason. Most actors were very firmly attached to studios by long-term contract. The studio production system is another reason. For economies of scale, studios kept their bulky equipment, set designers, carpenters, building materials, costumes, and creative people under one big roof, or on one big lot. By keeping everyone busy all the time, dividing their labor between several projects concurrently, the studios could crank out movies almost every week.

---

26. *Casablanca,* known for its all-star cast, had only three American-born actors in it, and the supporting cast is a veritable who's who of talent who had fled from Europe. Austrian, French, German and Hungarian refugees are represented both by the characters and the actors themselves, several of them only recently having escaped from Nazi persecution or even concentration camps. Several German actors were cast as Nazi officers, only too eager to show the true face of totalitarianism to western audiences.

To recreate such a logistical accomplishment in any other geographic area would have been formidable. Hollywood seemed immovable, permanent, and more powerful by the year. Each of the big studios owned theater chains. By forcing member theaters to book only films from one studio, it was very difficult for any small rivals to begin production outside Hollywood. In the early thirties, the U.S. government moved to break up the theater chains, but relented because of the hard times of a raging depression. Then the government relented again when World War II started.

HOLLYWOOD'S REALITY CHECK

The dreamy frivolity of Hollywood was only surpassed by its growing insulation from the real world. As America mobilized for the Second World War, American filmmakers and filmgoers were faced with the specter of an all-out conflict. The American government reached into Hollywood for contributions of ideas and idealism. The Office of War Information was created to better manage the contributions Tinsel Town could make, or could be persuaded to make, to the war effort. A number of actors abandoned the studios and enlisted as soldiers. John Ford was made chief of the Field Photographic Branch of the Office of Strategic Services. Ronald Reagan served as a Captain and Personnel Officer in the First Motion Picture Unit, which made more than four hundred films during the war, including Lt. Jimmy Stewart's *Winning Your Wings,* which was completed in fourteen days.

Walt Disney and other directors produced a number of public information films. Popular stars and comedians went on tours to entertain servicemen or sell war bonds. Frank Capra produced a weekly armed forces entertainment show, a "Know Your Allies—Know Your Enemies" serial, and most notably, the incredibly powerful "Why We Fight" series, which was instrumental in directly communicating American policy.

Hollywood's most esteemed cameramen followed troops into action and shot film for newsreels and records of the Army Signal Corps. Deep in the basement of Washington's National Archives Building, I've had the privilege of handling some of the very celluloid they loaded into their cameras and developed in the field. It is carefully stored and can be viewed on special 35mm flatbed projectors by making special appointment. Part of what this footage represents is production outside of Hollywood. The cameramen were resourceful as well as brave. It would be this resourcefulness and the gradual improvements of mobile film technologies that permitted more runaway productions after the war.

While many Hollywood professionals were involving themselves in the business of winning the war, the balance of Tinsel Town production was designed to raise spirits and morale through patriotic combat films, feel-good comedies, lively musicals, and other escapist fare to entertain and encourage the weary and worrying. When the war ended, a spate of similarly optimistic and cheery pictures tied into the return of our soldiers and the advent of peace.

As usual, the exception to this trend was European cynicism, this time from Italy. Dubbed the Neo-Realism movement, small studios and independent directors sprang up to fill the gaps in professional production caused by political meddling and bombing. Shooting with small crews and scrounged equipment, directors like Roberto Rossellini and Vittorio De Sica began shooting highly creative and simple stories, many of which explored new twists, or twisted old stories, into something of pessimistic ugliness.

What happened next in Hollywood was out of the American character. It was as if the entire industry went mad and started imitating the most ugly aspects of films that held no redeeming qualities. The deepest reasons for this will be discussed in the next chapter.

As Hollywood rapidly began to imitate the Euro-trends, the classic western, for example, became psychological and self-reflecting, with heroes and villains no longer separated by clear standards of right and wrong. *Film noir* came to the screen, a new genre which combined German expressionism with the formerly exciting gangster flick. Detective stories that had previously advocated justice and the triumph of the law now focused only on the crime, wallowing in violence and corruption. The cinematography was superlative, but the theology was warped and dark.

In 1948, the Supreme Court ordered the studios to sell their theaters, after they were found guilty of monopolization by the U.S. Justice Department. The smaller studios were eager to comply, hoping that the changes in business would leave them on equal footing with their more powerful competition. Supporting this change was the newly formed Society of Independent Motion Picture Producers.

Without the studio stranglehold on production, new types of films and new talent quickly appeared. On the downside, the independent producers who created the new films had no authority over them to keep budgets in check, shooting schedules short, and scripts audience-pleasing. This development helped to change the film industry from a purely money-making venture into a misunderstood blend of pretentious "art" and political education within a few short years. These years, the late forties and early fifties, were the pivotal years in Hollywood. The industry was sound in terms of professional ability. The country was upbeat and positive.

This could have been the dawning of a second Golden Age, more successful and constructive than the first. Instead, the leading films, many by more independent producers, followed the German trend toward pessimism, moral darkness, rebellion, and nihilism. Attendance dipped, but not by much, because Americans had become addicted to the silver screen. After a few years of this strange diet of political and psychological theology, American culture began to change. And thanks to a new army of filmgoers,[27] the culture changed rapidly.

BEHOLD THE GULLIBLE TEENAGER

Many of the children of post-war America were urban, idle, poorly educated, and confused by a post-war prosperity that had little to offer young people but alienation from success-oriented parents. Marlon Brando and James Dean acted in popular films that explained life to teen in these terms: *parental authority is irrelevant to modern life, rebellion and criticism are cool, and life has little real purpose.*

This set up an entire generation of impressionable American youth for immersion in a world of the media's making. The teens had the time for it, they had the disposable income to fund it, but they did not have the discernment to understand the ideas presented to them. The government school system was a ready pipeline for the culture of rebellion. Wild fashion, wild music, wild recreation came in a tsunami of pop culture that brought cultural upheaval.

The attitude of the day was represented in this famous exchange in the film *The Wild One* (1953). A girl asks Marlon Brando about the acronym on his motorcycle

27. While teens flocked to the theaters, older Americans were changing their habits and staying home. According to Michael Medved, it was not because of television but because Hollywood "opened floodgates to graphic sex, harsh language and intense violence." Medved reports the next decade witnessed the most dramatic audience decline in movie history: two billion annual admissions down to 920 million annual admissions. WorldNetDaily.com, July 1, 2002.

jacket.[28] "Black Rebels' Motorcycle Club," he says. She then asks, "What are you rebelling against?" He replies, "What have you got?"

As television became popular in the '50s, some film studios, like Paramount and Warner Brothers, embraced the new medium and began to create content for it. Others tried to make films of things television couldn't show, like wide-screen epics shot in full color, or daring, objectionable content that couldn't be legally broadcast.

A number of actors left their exclusive studio contracts to work on an individual project basis. Some started their own production companies or produced their own films. The sudden shift of authority away from the studios and the new interest in rebellious, irreverent films caused well-placed concern.

It was at this point that the U.S. House of Representatives Un-American Activities Committee began investigating subversive material in films and speculating about cultural subversives behind the cameras. The subversive ideas were apparent. But the subversive people were not willing to admit their ties to Marxist or Communist organizers, so the interviews with lying witnesses served little purpose but to play into the hands of media people outside of Hollywood, who used the occasion

---

28. Remembered by Gary North, *The War Against Mel Gibson*, Orphan Books, 2004.

to left-leaning political advantage.[29] By using a trick of the Hollywood screenwriter, the investigators were cast as the villains, and the Hollywood "artists" became the sympathetic characters,[30] and ultimately the heroes of a new and enduring mythology: *Communists are innocent and noble; American authorities are repressive, reactionary, and tyrannical.*

This mythology was so powerful that Hollywood has avoided any intelligent criticism of the communist world or its ideologies. According to film historian Lloyd Billingsley, "the major conflict of our time, democracy versus Marxist-Leninist totalitarianism—what *The New York Times* recently called 'the holy war of the 20th century'—is almost entirely missing from American cinema. It is as though since 1945, Hollywood had produced little or nothing about the victory of the Allies and the crimes of National Socialism. This void is all the stranger since the major conflict of our time would seem to be a natural draw for Hollywood."

It is curious that such a mercenary industry would value something more than the money that would come from a

---

29. According to Lloyd Billingsley, it didn't help matters that the first chairman of what became the committee was New York Democrat Samuel Dickstein. As the recently declassified "Venona" documents (decrypts of Soviet cables) reveal, Dickstein moonlighted for Soviet intelligence—not out of ideology but for money.

30. The so-called "Hollywood Ten," Alan Ryskind said, are usually presented as "victims of a terrible witchhunt, [but] that's not the case. They were basically agents of the Soviet Union—members of a party that was a wholly-owned subsidiary of [a government] which was out to subvert the United States." Quoted by L. Brent Bozell, "Communism in Hollywood—Still Making Believe," Creators Syndicate, November 5, 1997.

"natural draw." This is not rational. What made Hollywood
so irrational so suddenly, especially when it came to the
adoption of Marxist-Leninist totalitarianism?

Chapter 5

HOW HOLLYWOOD DESTROYED ITSELF

Hollywood was hardly a nursery for intellectuals, it was a hot-bed of false values. —David Niven [31]

In some film schools, 16mm cameras are issued to students along with a few short rolls of 16mm film. The students are meant to go out and put their creativity onto gorgeous high-contrast film, using the lessons and techniques learned in class. Some students are creative. They have stories to tell and seem to know how to tell them artistically and efficiently. Other students are, to put it politely, creatively challenged. They haven't a clue what to shoot. They don't have unlimited amounts of film. But they have an assignment with a deadline. Ask any film professor what these poor impostors shoot and they'll invariably tell you,

---

31. David Niven, *Bring on the Empty Horses*, p. 25.

"something with nudity... anything with nudity."

During the early years of experimental industry growth, some opportunistic Hollywood entrepreneurs were also idea-poor. Looking for commercial value and intense visual interest, they experimented with the disrobed female form. This was nothing more than opportunism, a move to make a faster buck than the other guy with a camera. The more responsible studios knew these cheap thrills could be bad for the industry as a whole, and created self-regulating customs in an effort to drive gratuitous opportunism into a different outlet. The customs were voluntarily followed by the leading studios of the '20s, who encouraged others to sign-on to the Motion Picture Production Code which was published in 1930. Observe the tone of moral responsibility in the preamble to the code:

> Motion picture producers recognize the high trust and confidence which have been placed in them by the people of the world and which have made motion pictures a universal form of entertainment.
>
> They recognize their responsibility to the public because of this trust and because entertainment and art are important influences in the life of a nation.
>
> Hence, though regarding motion pictures as entertainment without an explicit purpose for teaching or propaganda, they know that the motion picture within its own field of entertainment may be directly responsible for spiritual or moral progress, for higher types of social life, and for much correct thinking.

Today this language would only appear in Hollywood as a scriptwriter's spoof. Something happened to the Hollywood of Mary Pickford's era. The idea of "correct thinking" is still in the Hollywood vocabulary, but it has a new meaning, which is brazenly political.

This is because Hollywood was politicized, beginning in the 1930s. The tightly-knit Hollywood community of artists and businessmen began to move away from morally-correct thinking to politically-correct thinking. Hollywood now celebrates, on film, political concepts like moral experimentation, moral diversity, sexual liberation, social engineering, behavioral psychology, institutional pessimism, cultural terror, selective tolerance, and political correctness. There is an important point that needs to be made about Hollywood's obsession with all this malevolence. This isn't market opportunism today and it wasn't in the '50s and '60s. Hollywood simply became enamored of political and cultural powers of manipulation. They discovered they could be politically influential. They discovered they could be politically correct. They discovered they could change the thinking of politically incorrect people, the world over, by using moral derangement, aesthetic disintegration, and cultural terrorism in movie content.

Many Hollywood professionals now consider it a social duty on their part to correct the thinking of their less fortunate public. Furthermore, they think we should be grateful to them for passing on some of their coolness to us.

Says George Clooney, "As an actor in the public eye, I have a responsibility. I see myself as a spokesman for all those who have the same opinion."[32] Hollywood insiders are conscientious conformists. The heartbeat of their ideology is nothing more than consistent, fashionable, relentless criticism of all things traditional, especially the "the dangerous right-wing agenda," as Ben Affleck states it,[33] or "all those old fashioned values," as Madonna prefers to describe them.[37]

These hyper-critical Hollywood insiders are not only on the same ideological page, but specific attitudes of arrogant superiority are widely used to make that ideology culturally dominant: repressive intolerance, denigration, aggressive humiliation, and hatred toward certain people or classes of people. People who disagree can find themselves shut up in a politically correct cage. Conformist Alec Baldwin complains that the Left is not critical enough: "[...it's] too tolerant, too open-minded, not feral enough... I want to be the ferocious liberal."[34]

POLITICALLY IRRATIONAL ENTERTAINMENT

It would be almost funny if the stupidity wasn't so serious and so seriously self-perpetuating. Comedian Chevy Chase wasn't joking when he said Cuba is proof that socialism

---

32. Yahoo.com News, October 22, 2003.

33. *New York Daily News*, October 16, 2003.

34. *corsinet.com*, 1992. Madonna claimed her rebellion against these values "made" her what she was.

works. He was deadly serious, and deadly dishonest, about a tyranny that enslaves people politically against their will. This is not funny, but it is the face of the politically correct stupor in which Hollywood operates.

How does Hollywood perpetuate and spread an internal culture that is so stupid it doesn't even know it's stupid? This is part of the mystery and genius of Hollywood culture. Tinsel Town not only perpetuates itself, it perpetuates a very specific ideological identity.

The new heart and soul of Hollywood is not made up of ditzy actors, trainers, and plastic surgeons. It is made up of writers, journalists, producers, columnists, agents, professional gossips, publicists, and lawyers. These people are not unintelligent, but they maintain a level of self-deception that surpasses that of the dizziest celebrities.[35] How? They seem to exist on a kind of energy that makes Hollywood a perpetual-motion machine. That energy is ideology, and it inspires the insiders to maintain Hollywood as a self-policing gulag of self-congratulatory leftist narcissism. Every

---

35. People joke about Hollywood's legendary aversion to honesty because celebrities have turned self-deception into an art form. Nobody gets "old" and nobody ever becomes a "nobody." *Every insider is a star, forever and ever.* According to Goldie Hawn, insiders use code words when speaking about the age of an actress. She's a "babe" if she's younger, "Miss Daisy" if she's older, and "District Attorney" if she's somewhere in between. Unfortunately, this silly deception also extends to the morality of insiders. "What used to be called shame and humiliation is now called publicity," writes P.J. O'Rourke in *Give War a Chance.* "If you say a modern celebrity is an adulterer, a pervert and a drug addict, all it means is that you've read his autobiography."

project, every party, every billboard, and even the food in the restaurants seems to nourish an immortal fraternity of harmful ideology. It is this pseudo-intellectual fraternity that manages the ideas that determine how filmgoers think.

Other books have documented the fact that that the Hollywood ideology is narcissistic Leftist *supremacy*. What I find hard to understand is how such a bankrupt, discredited ideology can survive so strongly in Hollywood. I suppose the Left can't be wrong because it is supremely correct, by definition. This is the essence of ideology. The Right is always wrong and always will be. No one in Hollywood can be politically *in*correct because, well, first of all, it's not cool and, secondly, there's no energy to sustain political incorrectness. The limelight is on correctness, for perpetuity. Hollywood considers itself the guardian of the limelight and it only has candlepower for correctness. Nothing exists outside the brilliance of this limelight, and insiders tap-dance, as Sharon Stone put it, on pedestals.

INVERTING THE CULTURE AND TURNING THE WORLD UPSIDE DOWN

"They stand astride the most powerful media instrument of all time," says Ben Stein about these enthusiasts. "This tiny community in Hollywood has been given the fulcrum that can move the world—and its members know how to use it." In the late '70s, Hollywood outsider Stein[36] went to

---

36. Today the former Yale Law graduate and presidential speechwriter is a Hollywood insider, a veteran actor of some forty film and television productions.

Hollywood to have a look inside. His findings became an insightful book titled *The View from Sunset Boulevard*.

Stein discovered there are only a couple of hundred insiders who decide what Americans watch on television, and by analyzing the popular shows, he profiled this group politically. Stein documented how various social groups are consistently scripted: businessmen (as criminals), the military (psychotic sadists), minorities of all descriptions (good-hearted), small towns (evil), criminals (victims of racism and poverty), clergy (uninformed, unsophisticated, ineffectual), government social workers (noble, idealistic, hard-working). Also noted were the recurrent themes involving the stupidity of fathers, the children who know better than their parents, the liberated female who rejects motherhood, above all the responsibility of the white male for all that is wrong with the world.

In short, these television people are dedicated to loading political correctness into every script, and every script has its villains—and those villains must be traditionalists, consistently Christian traditionalists. This is the worldview from Sunset Boulevard.[37] In an effort to understand the cause for such a contrived opinion, Stein came up with an answer

---

37. Donald Bellisario, who produced such television series as *Magnum P.I.*, *Quantum Leap*, and *JAG*, stated that, "There's only two classes of people you can portray as a villain on a television action-adventure show anymore, and that would be the Russians or white, middle-class Americans." Dan Roodt, "Hollywood lunges for white South Africa," WorldNetDaily.com, August 7, 2004.

that must be used in any analysis of Hollywood's political irrationality.

"It all came together for me only by using a Marxian analysis," Stein writes. "The TV people are now in a position to dominate society. They can contend with the businessman class, with the military class, with small town gentry, with anyone for the leadership role in society. But they realize that [these traditional] power centers must be denigrated and humiliated if they are to take the top positions."[38]

This is the warlike attitude, inspired by a militant Marxist worldview, which has captivated not just the mentality of the Hollywood insider, but also the professional agenda of the industry. Every aspiring filmmaker needs to use a Marxian analysis, as Ben Stein did, if he is to understand the dangers of the industry, its errors, and its commitment to ongoing irrationality and political correctness. What characteristics of the Marxist worldview[39] are obviously present in Hollywood today?

- A herd-mentality, with dependency on politically-correct comradeship

- A fear of being incorrect

---

38. Ibid.

39. Marx's worldview is explained in "The German Ideology" of 1845, in which he expands on his War Plan of 1843, revealing his process for the disintegration of the middle class and his castigation of the family as the basic unit of society.

- A confidence in the superiority of Hollywood's political culture

- A cold intolerance to differing viewpoints

- A loathing of a consistent high moral standard

- A bitterness toward a traditional environment that has allegedly wronged them

- An aggrieved mentality

- An imaginary sympathy with all other victims of white, male, Euro-centric culture

- An emancipator mentality, with the aggressive urge to force therapy on the psychologically inferior

- A fervent faith in the science of behavioral psychology

- A quick willingness to endorse totalitarian means to change culture

- A pessimistic distrust of European Christendom

- A bold attraction to every liberating idea, especially sexual license

- A bold dedication to shred the envelope of on-screen decency

- A strong desire to alienate others from all things traditional

- A sophisticated affinity for leftist politics and a hatred of conservative ideas

- A realization that the sting of vindictive criticism must be light enough that viewers accept it.

How did these militant characteristics so thoroughly captivate Hollywood? How is it that Marxism can so cleverly replace clear thinking with politicized blindness? It didn't happen overnight.

THE ORIGINS OF HOLLYWOOD'S HYPER-CRITICAL CRUELTY

To apply a Marxian analysis to Hollywood, one needs to first understand Karl Marx. To put Marx in historical context, he was a contemporary of Abe Lincoln, living in Europe. Historian Robert Wistrich states that Marx was primarily "engaged in an assault on the religious foundations of the Christian state of Prussia."[40] That is a fair summary, but incomplete. Marx wanted Christianity dead in every nation. Marx was known as a Christian in his youth. Probably in his nineteenth year, he suddenly turned his back on any loyalty he had to the Christian faith, and transferred all his energy into efforts to destroy the faith and any attached institutions, including Western civilization itself. His hatred was incalculable. It is said Marx sold his very soul to Satan, to whom he later wrote passionate poetry.

---

40. Karl Marx from *Oulanem*. Even in his own lifetime, Karl Marx attempted to apply his theories in revolutionary action. When Marx published the *Communist Manifesto* in 1848, he was a leader of the Communist League. However, these early communists failed in their revolutionary attempt. Marx fled into exile and wrote *Das Kapital* (1867) and other works.

Soon I shall embrace eternity to my breast,
and soon I shall howl gigantic curses on mankind...
If there is a something which devours,
I'll leap within it,
though I bring the world to ruins.
The world which bulks between me and the abyss
I will smash to pieces with my enduring curses...
Behold this sword—the prince of darkness sold it to me.
For he beats the time and gives the signs.
Ever more boldly I play the dance of death.[41]

Marx was also big fan of the developing pseudo-science of phrenology,[42] which was later re-branded by its proponents as "psychology." Right in Marx's backyard, behavioral psychology was perfected as a "social science" to be used for purposes of social engineering.[43] Marx believed revolutionary cultural disintegration was the real muscle of this social science, and would succeed in the destruction of all Christendom.

Marx himself shaped a practice of destructive, ruthless criticism. "But war on the state of affairs in Germany...

41. Robert Payne, *The Unknown Karl Marx,* London, 1972, p. 81.

42. "Phrenologists" believed they could examine bumps on human skulls and determine deep truths about people's souls, and even foretell personality strengths and character weaknesses. These findings could be used to engineer human interactions, prescribing where people should fit into society.

43. By the 1850s, Germany had the reputation of being the scientific center of the world, especially in the ability to redefine non-scientific matters into scientific ones. By the 1870s, the University of Leipzig's psychology laboratories became the world center of the idea that man is nothing more than a stimulus-response mechanism.

criticism... is not a lancet but a weapon. Its object is an enemy which it aims not to refute but to destroy." He also wrote, "the criticism of religion is the premise of all criticism. The nation must be taught to be terrified of itself."

Marx didn't live long enough to see his great enemy, Christendom, fully destroyed. He had predicted that blue-collar workers could be made so enraged with Christian-capitalist society that they would unite across national boundaries as they destroyed their governments and flocked to an international socialist utopia. This didn't happen. Even during World War I, working men preferred their fatherlands to international solidarity.

However, in 1917, a follower of Marx saw opportunity in the chaos of World War I. By slandering the rulers of other nations, Vladimir Lenin forced a revolution on Russia, which at that time had one of the fastest growing economies in the world. Lenin's uprising seemed to be working, but not because Russian workers were eagerly following Marxist principles. It worked because of Lenin's total choke-hold on the police-state and ruthless policy of social control. Lenin insisted on political correctness from everyone, on pain of death. There was a lot of death, inflicted by the state in the name of the people. Lenin used bullets for short-term solutions, and employed State propaganda and forced-schooling to ensure long-term compliance.[44]

---

44. In one famous quote, Lenin boasted, "Through the schools we will transform the old world... the final victory will belong to the schools... the final sketch plan of the socialist society will belong to the schools."

Throughout Europe, the students of Marx rejoiced, and in 1919 the Communist Internationale, or Comintern, was organized to oversee the spread of the revolution worldwide. Germany and Hungary were targeted next, but the revolutions in Berlin, Bavaria, and Hungary[45] didn't succeed, not even at the point of bayonet. This left the Comintern vanguard puzzled.

Some of the Communist Internationale's best minds gathered in the early '20s to figure out what was wrong. Marx had predicted cascading victories. Lenin thought the time was right. Why were the workers of the world not gathering to the party? Why could they not see the superiority of a utopian system that crushed all individual liberty, abolished private property, and enforced standards of political correctness for the glory of a messianic state? The leader of the Comintern suggested a change in strategy.

GEORG AND HIS FERVENT DISCIPLES

Georg Lukacs had earned his stripes as a progressive minister of culture in the brand new Hungarian communist government of 1919. He called his political agenda "cultural terror," and he went about it systematically until he felt the fury of Hungarian Christians when he tried to force

---

45. There was a Communist Spartacist uprising in Berlin, Germany, led by Rosa Luxemburg; the creation of a Bavarian Soviet in Germany led by Kurt Eisner, and a Hungarian Soviet established by Bella Kun in 1919. At the time, there was great concern that all of Europe might soon fall under the banner of Bolshevism. But each of these three revolutions was turned back within months, primarily by private citizens.

his version of sex education into Hungarian schools.[46] The parents objected, and Lukacs had to flee for his life under cover of darkness. That's how the Hungarian communist government fell apart before 1920; families flatly rejected it because of the threats it posed to their children.

It was not difficult for Lukacs to convince a cadre of other bright operatives the revolution needed an amended strategy.[47] His rallying cry was, "...who will save us from Western civilization!?" With Christendom out of the way, people all over the West would more readily settle for the messianic political order of the socialist state, he concluded.

---

46. Lukac's curriculum contained graphic information about the nature of sexual intercourse, about the archaic nature of the bourgeois family codes, about the outdatedness of monogamy, and the irrelevance of religion, which the Marxists said deprives man of all pleasures. Children thus urged to reject and deride paternal authority and the authority of the Church, and to ignore precepts of morality, easily and spontaneously turned into delinquents with whom only the police could cope. Delinquency and chaos was Lukacs' goal. This call to rebellion addressed to Hungarian children was matched by a call to rebellion addressed to Hungarian women.

47. In 1922, Lukacs was deployed by Moscow to Germany, the perfect academic center for the popularizing of this new social science. Collaborators included Karl Korsh, Karl Wittfogel, and Soviet spymasters Richard Sorge and Antonio Gramsci. Later members of the Frankfurt School included Nathan Ackerman, Theodor Adorno (born Wiesengrund), Walter Benjamin, Bruno Bettelheim, Ernst Bloch, Erich Fromm, Carl Gruenberg, Julian Gumperz, Max Horkheimer, Otto Kirchheimer, Leo Lowenthal, Kurt Mandelbaum, Herbert Marcuse, Franz Neumann, Friedrich Pollock, Ernst Schachtel, Adries Sternheim, and Karl Wittfogel. Wittfogel, the son of a Lutheran pastor, broke with Marxism after coming to America and testified against the communists before the U.S. Senate. Wittfogel is best known for his analysis of communism, *Oriental Despotism*.

So these front-line revolutionaries traded their jackboots and government desks for academic titles and went to work on the strategies for this cultural revolution at a think-tank they created and attached to the University of Frankfurt in Germany.

Originally called the *Institute for the Study of Marxism*, their name was altered to a more circumspect *Institute for Social Research*. They published scores of "scientific" papers on such topics as why "matriarchy was the only genuine family type of 'natural society.'" These published initiatives are chilling. Their unpublished strategies are even more so. B. K. Eakman calls the Frankfurt School "far and away the most successful psychological warfare operation ever launched against the West."[48]

BUILDING THE IRON CAGE

Marxian analysis is imperative in understanding what happened to Hollywood. None of this can be understood without understanding that Marx was a dedicated fighter. He was at war. He needed blood in the streets for his revolution of chaos to succeed. His followers, like Lukacs, only amended Marx's strategies to fight smarter and more ruthlessly. Marx intended the bloody conflict to take place between the rich and the poor. When "the poor" turned out to have too many Christian scruples to murder the rich, Lukacs and his contemporaries realized the need

---

48. B.K. Eakman, *The Coming of the American Mind* (Lafayette: Huntington House, 1998), p. 147.

for a new battle with different combatants: *"politically literate" revolutionaries vs. Christian patriarchs.* In order to win the war, Lukacs needed to create a superior force of blindly submissive, politically-correct hotheads with the "revolutionary personality."

"Until man is convinced that the world has been abandoned by God," said Lukacs, "there will be no revolution." To prove abandonment, Lukacs planned the destruction of civil society by making it terrifyingly uncivil. "I saw the revolutionary destruction of society as the one and only solution to the cultural contradictions of the epoch," he explained. This is what Lukacs was writing. His real intentions were disclosed by one of his comrades named Antonio Gramsci.

Comintern agent Antonio Gramsci worked closely on the strategies of Neo-Marxism from Moscow and Vienna in 1923-4. He showed how the use of mass psychology to break the traditions, beliefs, morals, and will of a people could be accomplished without resistance. He deduced that "The civilized world had been thoroughly saturated with Christianity for 2,000 years...", and a culture based on this religion could only be captured from within.

A RELIGIOUSLY FERVENT CULT OF EVIL

The cultural doctrine developed by Lukacs and his team of propagandists was perfectly suited for Hollywood's media culture and the medium of filmmaking. Vice would be made trendy, then popular, then required. In keeping with Lenin's mandate to include a forced-schooling curriculum, the Frankfurt School developed the material for both classroom and silver screen. Lukacs worked on a "demonically energetic" political movement to reorder "a world that has been abandoned by God," to "aufhebung der Kultur" (abolish culture) through "cultural pessimism." Hollywood would become the Sensuality Cartel, creating a delinquent people dependent on demoralizing entertainment.[49] Government schools would become the Illiteracy Cartel, and would be run worldwide by Lukacs' own behavioral psychologists.

And so, Lukacs' Frankfurt School colleagues played their roles and were brilliantly radical and outspoken for decades. Their publications were not vague about their aims to demoralize the West. Walter Benjamin threw out the concept of good and evil and defended Satanism and "the cult of evil" as beneficial tools for subverting traditional culture. He advised, "Do not build on the good old days, but on the bad new ones."

---

49. "We are obliged…to [make] amusement a weapon of collective education. The cinema competes…with the church. This rivalry may become fatal for the church if we make up for the separation of the church from the socialist state by the fusion of the socialist state and the cinema. The cinema…liberates you from the need of crossing the church door. Here is an instrument which we must secure at all costs!" Leon Trotsky, *Pravda*, July 12, 1923

RESURRECTING JEZEBEL

In 1925, an article about the influence of Hollywood appeared in a newspaper called the *Daily Worker*, the organ of the Communist party. "One of the most pressing tasks confronting the Communist Party in the field of propaganda," wrote Comintern agent Willi Muenzenberg, "is the conquest of this supremely important propaganda unit, until now the monopoly of the ruling class. We must wrest it from them and turn it against them."[50]

At first glance, the quote looks like typical rhetorical boosterism from dissatisfied political underdogs. But by 1925, the Comintern had developed a general plan for not only seizing Hollywood, but also making it glamorize *cultural terror*. Lukacs and his intellectual propagandists had no doubt that the media was the fulcrum that would change culture.[51] Hollywood was to be the doomsday machine in

---

50. Kenneth Lloyd Billingsley, "Hollywood's Missing Movies — Why American films have ignored life under communism" *freerepublic.com*, June 8, 2000.

51. Most of my information on Frankfurt School writers is derived from research my father conducted prior to lecturing on the Frankfurt School's policies of Critical Theory at Hillsdale College in the mid 1990s. I know he, in turn, is indebted to many colleagues with whom he consulted to assemble the research, including Ray V. Raehn, retired Naval officer and think-tank chairman; William Lind, fourth-generation-warfare specialist with the Free Congress Foundation; B.K. Eakman of the National Education Consortium and author of the book *The Coming of the American Mind* (Huntington House, 1998); economist Dr. Gary North, author of *Marx's Religion of Revolution* (Institute for Christian Economics, 1968, 1989); John Taylor Gatto, author of *An Underground History of American Education*; and national

the Marxian struggle to destroy Christendom and replace it
with a culture of ferocious pessimism.

In 1935, V.J. Jerome, the Communist Party's United
States cultural commissar, set up a Hollywood branch of
the party. This highly secretive unit enjoyed great success,
according to Lloyd Billingsley, "recruiting members,
organizing entire unions, raising money from unwitting
Hollywood liberals, and using those funds to support Soviet
causes through front groups such as the Hollywood Anti-
Nazi League."[52]

One associate of Lukacs is said to have adopted ancient
Babylon as the ideal model culture and civilization, in
opposition to that of Judeo-Christian Europe. This Freudian
remarked, "if Jezebel had not been defeated by Elijah, world
history would have been different and better. Jezebel was
Babylon. By killing her, Jewish monotheistic moralism drove
pleasure from the world."[53] The solution of the Frankfurt
School was "to start a sexual revolution and destroy the
bourgeois, patriarchal family."[54]

Screenwriter-Director Philip Dunne said, "All over
town the industrious communist tail wagged the lazy

---

security affairs analyst Dr. Joseph D. Douglass.

52. Kenneth Lloyd Billingsley, "Hollywood's Missing Movies — Why
American films have ignored life under communism," *freerepublic.com*, June
8, 2000.

53. Michael Minnicino, writing of psychoanalyst Otto Gross in "The New
Dark Age," *Fidelio*, Winter, 1992, p. 6.

54. Ibid., p. 7.

liberal dog."[55] As former Communist party member Budd
Schulberg (*On the Waterfront*) described the Hollywood
of later years, the Communist party was "the only game
in town."[56]

Lukacs' cultural revolution was working, and by 1940,
it was no longer politically incorrect to be sympathetic
to cultural demoralization. Lukacs was a genius at public
relations. He sold cultural disintegration as intellectual
charm and polish. There was a cosmopolitan mystique about
it all, especially the intellectualized German variety that was
coming out of the Frankfurt School. Who in Hollywood
would have wanted to appear too shallow to appreciate
German intellectualism?

By the early forties, America was less infatuated with
Germany, and was soon allied with Stalin's Soviet Union.
Lenin, who once said the American capitalists would sell
him the rope with which he would hang them, might now
have said, "Hollywood moguls will now fund the films that
will disintegrate their entire culture." Criticism of the Soviet
propaganda effort was muted. Billingsley finds that the
Comintern's Hollywood "artists in uniform" were not greatly
successful in making movies with the new political religion,[57]

---

55. Quoted by Billingsley, from Dunne's 1980 memoir, *Take Two: A Life in
Movies and Politics*.

56. Billingsley, "Hollywood's Missing Movies."

57. Billingsley does cite at least two, however. Wartime movies *North Star*
and *Song of Russia* (both 1943), portrayed the USSR as a land of joyous, well-
fed workers who loved their masters.

but that they were very successful in killing productions that were critical of Soviet propaganda and Frankfurt School ideas.[58]

Meanwhile, the cult of evil continued to poison Hollywood culture. Lukacs and his disciples had moved to the United States as refugees, and were plugging themselves into choice media and educational positions from Columbia Teachers College to Hollywood.

A quick summary of these men and their teachings is an alarming look at the culture of demoralization they were successfully pushing, both in Hollywood and in leading colleges.[59]

Lukacs was convinced that to prepare society for psychological control, the very soul of the individual must be destroyed in its youth by disturbing it with evil via school and media. "One must act immorally in order to transform evil into good—by doing evil things you accomplish the good," he said. He also subscribed to the Marxian dictum that revolutionary cultural disintegration is the new social science which will save all nations from Christendom.

---

58. According to Billingsley, communist scriptwriter Dalton Trumbo openly bragged that the following works had not reached the screen: Arthur Koestler's *Darkness at Noon* and *The Yogi and the Commissar*; Victor Kravchenko's *I Chose Freedom*; and *Bernard Clare* by James T. Farrell.

59. The University of Chicago and Columbia Teachers College were two top destinations. Educator John Dewey's protégé at Columbia arranged the mass migration of Frankfurt School personnel from Germany to the U.S. in the thirties. He, too, became a fan of Frankfurt School propaganda techniques and later went to work at CBS under the name Edward R. Murrow.

Sigmund Freud reckoned man an irrational, unthinking, immoral sex animal with no possible connection to a Creator, who has abandoned society to a new god—the State—which can engineer society far better than any divinity.

Kurt Lewin believed that traditional behavior could be *artificially disorganized* by operant conditioning, sensitivity training, cognitive dissonance, and other non-academic classroom exercises.

Wilhelm Reich believed the key to destroying the family is destroying the father's authority, "to dethrone the patriarchal power in man."[60] He equated patriarchy with fascism.

Erich Fromm, the creator of gender politics, taught that the classroom must separate the good people from the bad. The bad are the traditionalists, the good are those who "make war against ties of blood, soil, mother, father and religion." He also believed the very character traits of traditionalists, especially patriarchs, must be criminalized.[61]

Herbert Marcuse developed the concept of "liberating tolerance." This is deliberate *in*tolerance of the Right,

---

60. R.V. Raehn, "The Roots of Affective Education in American Schools," unpublished research report, March 1, 1995. p. 8.

61. According to R.V. Raehn, the belief in patriarchy is to be inverted to a belief in matriarchy in accordance with Frankfurt School matriarchal theory. The belief in distinct gender roles is to be inverted to a belief that distinct gender roles should not exist in accordance with Frankfurt School androgyny theory.

and a prime component of political correctness, and the intimidating forces that push traditionalists, cowed, into the psychic iron cage, where they can no longer object to the inversion of culture. Marcuse is considered the granddaddy of the sixties' sex, drugs, and rock culture.

Theodore Adorno praised cultural forces that destroyed the creative thinking potential of whole generations of Americans. "Techniques for overcoming resistance [to political correctness]," he wrote, "developed mainly in the field of individual psychotherapy, can be improved and adopted for use with groups and even for use on a mass scale."[62]

Adorno actually cataloged the psychiatric and neurological disorders that could be induced by steady exposure to top-forty music hits. The unspeakable barbarity of the today's top-forty rap hits about drugs, thugs, pimping, and recreational rape is exactly what the Frankfurt School faculty was aiming for: Lukacs' vision of cultural terrorism. From its pinnacle position in the art world, Hollywood was influencing radio, television, music, and the fine arts world.

Artists were getting the politically correct message and were falling into line. "Modern art," said the museum

---

62. The late Christopher Lasch used these words when describing the Frankfurt School plan for eliminating the patriarchal mindset. "[It] could be eradicated only by subjecting the American people to what amounted to collective psychotherapy—by treating them as inmates of an insane asylum." Quoted by Geoffrey Botkin, "Critical Theory and the Institute for Social Research," Hillsdale College Lecture series, 1998.

director of a famous design school, "has nothing to do with aesthetics, craftsmanship, or design. Its purpose is to "challenge us. It demands that we rethink our assumption about every issue of life."[63] A biographer of crass modern artists went further, praising modern artists with these words, "their lyricism celebrated... iron Bolshevik discipline, revolutionary ruthlessness, merciless struggle against religion, total overthrow of all... Christian values and institutions."[64]

This compliment precisely describes the art of late twentieth century Hollywood. Lukacs had succeeded, and Lenin had been right. The motion picture was the most important of all the arts. Hollywood had been transformed. The new mentality was indeed merciless. Political incorrectness within Hollywood and without would never again be tolerated.

Few observers realize the extent to which these ideas attained dominion in America's academic and entertainment circles. By carefully importing these destructive ideas into Hollywood during its formative years, the thirties and forties, the Frankfurt School "socialized" Hollywood. Hollywood was introduced to the new social mind. The new virtues. The new political correctness.

In 1949, the Tavistock Institute declared, "it is now possible from one source to influence the thinking of

---

63. Hamilton Reed Armstrong, quoting Franklin Robinson of the Rhode Island School of Design. *The Role of Art in Society*, The American Cause, 1994, p. 9.

64. Ibid., p. 10.

hundreds of millions of people."[65] By 1950, Hollywood was ready to spread the word while perpetuating a tightly-knit, elitist "insider" culture. Since the 1960s, Hollywood has done this with religious fervor.

Christians are vilified, patriarchy is condemned, old virtues ridiculed, and patriotism has become *verboten*. These new customs will be enforced both on the screen and off, which is why the priesthood of the new media preserves this fundamentalist criticism with passion and fidelity. Nothing must ever be allowed to reveal any other reality than what stands proudly in this rose-tinted limelight. If the liturgy of this religious fervor sounds sanctimonious, that's because it is. "The United States is a stupid, aggressive puppy," says a sacerdotal Johnny Depp.[66] "I regret what we as a country have done so far," obliges Harrison Ford, in speaking about the same nation.[67]

When actor Ed Asner was asked about the one historic figure he would most like to portray, the answer was easy. "I think Joe Stalin was a guy that was hugely misunderstood," he said,[68] which raises a chilling possibility. If Stalin is understood by Asner and not the public, does that mean Asner wants to lionize the man who took great delight in the propagandizing of Hollywood? Would Asner restate

---

65. Eakman, p. 144. A psycho-political think-tank and training center in Britain.

66. *Stern* magazine, September 2, 2003.

67. *The Age*, August 31, 2003.

68. WorldNetDaily.com, October 10, 2003.

the words[69] Stalin used before the Politburo in 1939? There Stalin urged policies that would unite Russia with Nazi Germany to create a "major war" which would be extended "as long as possible" so the armies and police of the Western powers could be demoralized, that Poland could be totally destroyed, and that an international arena could be created for the propagandizing of the Western powers. "We must step up our propaganda," Stalin raged, "in order to be prepared when the war ends!"

By the time the war ended, Georg Lukacs and his disciples had made this destructive criticism seem very trendy. They had created hundreds of semi-sophisticated followers in Hollywood who understood little but that society must come down. "They no longer believed really in the future," observes David Horowitz. "They believed only in destroying."[70]

When a doctrine like this gets out of control in the most important media center in the world, the industry itself goes out of control. Media analyst Brent Bozell reviewed the television series titled *Nip/Tuck,* which is known for graphic celebrations of sexual perversion. "If... this is the direction 'cool' TV is going," asks Bozell, "if this is 'the future,' then where will Hollywood stop? Where is the

69. Speech delivered on August 19, 1939. Albert Weeks: *Stalin's Other War: Soviet Grand Strategy 1939-1941* (Rowman & Littlefield, 2003), p. 171-173.

70. David Horowitz, president of the Center for the Study of Popular Culture, in *The Frankfurt School*, a documentary produced by the National Empowerment Network, 1998.

bottom of the barrel located, or is our desire for 'fabulously lurid' entertainment a bottomless pit of nihilism? *Nip/Tuck* is not just a show that's completely inappropriate for impressionable children to watch. It's a show adults should be convincing other adults not to support. The sanity of our popular culture depends on our objections."[71]

In answer to Bozell's question, there is no bottom of the barrel. According to the wishes and goals of Frankfurt School strategists, Hollywood is becoming a bottomless pit of nihilism and pessimism. The new Hollywood has been designed to destroy sanity, culture, tradition, manners, morals, and the very heart of civilization, the nuclear family. It also exists to mute any objections from those, insider or not, who would attempt to challenge Hollywood's established elitist ideology of what is acceptable.

---

71. Brent Bozell, "'Nip/Tuck' knows no bounds," Creator's Syndicate, August 20, 2004.

Chapter 6

COWARDLY FILMMAKING

*Hollywood people lived and still live in a world of
fantasy, and they are accustomed to making things up,
to fibbing and exaggerating, and to believing all their
own fibs and exaggerations.   —Otto Friederich* [72]

As a concerned grandfather, businessman Philip F.
Anschutz recently launched himself into the movie
business in an effort to make films that families could view
together. As a new executive member of the Academy of
Motion Picture Arts and Sciences, he has seen the movie
business up close and has identified elements of what he calls
the Hollywood mindset. "One of these," he reports, "is that
the way to be successful is to be hip and edgy.... Another
is that you have to grow up in the film business in order
to understand it and have the right creative instincts for it.
Another is that to earn respect from your peers within the

---

72. Otto Frederich, *City of Nets* (New York: Harper and Row, 1986), p. xiii.

Hollywood community, you have to make at least potential Academy Award films—which in recent history have predominantly been R-rated."[73]

Anschutz has described the politically-correct mindset, which is a cowardly mindset. This explains why Hollywood doesn't break out of the self-perpetuating political correctness established by the neo-Marxists in the 1940s. The cowards of Hollywood make themselves comfortable inside purely because the other influential people are inside. The proper "instincts" require the Hollywood insider to comply with all that is politically correct. This is what it means to be "hip."' Filmmakers are perpetually trying to please their peers with their political sophistication, which is nothing more than chronic, cowardly conformity to the entrenched ideology.

One would expect independent filmmakers to be different, but moral courage is rarely seen. Industry approval is an attractive prize, and most independents' only goal is to be accepted in the standard "rich and famous" world of Hollywood's celebrities.

Today's politically-correct Hollywood is so committed to the precepts of the humanistic message that there is no more room for honesty or virtue. Truth is off limits, even when a film needs it. And usually, we expect nothing more of

73. Philip F. Anschutz , February 24, 2004, at a Hillsdale National Leadership Seminar in Naples, Florida, upon receipt by Mr. Anschutz of the Adam Smith Award from Hillsdale College.

them. Even if we miss the covert worldviews that undergird blockbusters today, it is painfully easy to spot overt anti-Christian and anti-family messages in almost every major Hollywood production. The ideas that the Communist writers of the '50s tried so hard to hide are today plastered across the advertising posters.

But what about Christian filmmaking? If they can avoid falling into the obvious ideological pits, can they also refute Hollywood's more subtle worldview? With few exceptions, films made by Christians are a frustrating mixture of ideological conformity and poor production quality. Gary North explains some reasons behind this peculiarity:

> For well over a hundred years, Christians in the United States have been absent without leave in this civilization. They have distinguished themselves in no field except linguistics: Bible translation. They have told themselves that culture is irrelevant, and they have watched their children seduced by it. They have told themselves that the Bible is silent about culture, which means that Satan speaks the only words of cultural truth. For decades, they insisted that the best way to deal with American culture is to build a cultural wall around their families. Then they went out and bought radios and television sets and stereos and VCRs.[74]

Christians have willingly immersed themselves in the filmmaking culture of a politically captive Hollywood. Without a robust worldview or solid theology to understand

---

74. Gary North, *The War Against Mel Gibson* (Orphan Books, 2004).

the ways the Bible speaks about culture, most aspiring Christian filmmakers make what can only be described as cowardly films. Their films contain all the bad ideas of secular film, which harm Christian viewers, and then they add some sort of tacky, easy-gospel propaganda, which harms other viewers.

Here is a sad example of this lose-lose strategy: On several occasions, my father has been asked by Christian film producers for advice on packaging projects for the screen. In the most recent case, he patiently explained the production process for turning a true story into a feature film. From a purely commercial point of view, the story in question could be presented in any one of eight different ways. My father explained the eight genres that would fit the facts of the story, then presented eight completely different treatments,[75] pointing out that three would be superior, four inferior, and one so self-contradicting that "...your enemies would be proud to see it brought to the screen."

Asked to choose the one treatment that would best represent truth to millions of impressionable people, the producer contemplated each one carefully, then enthusiastically picked *the very worst*, not having the discernment to see the dangers in such an injudicious

---

75. A "treatment" is a summary of the way a film would be handled, containing information about the style, story content, genre, plot, characters, and directorial approach. Hollywood treatments are usually submitted in one, four, and twelve-page formats. A "log-line" is a one or two-sentence description of a film.

handling of the truth. It so happened that the worst one was the one most like the version Hollywood would make. With any film, this is the easiest course to take, the one requiring the least amount of courage, creativity, or discernment.

In another situation, my father was asked to provide some "Christian" content for a children's series. One of my father's suggestions was rejected because it was simply too virtuous. The producer was uncomfortable with the virtue that was being displayed. He simply wanted some worldly content that had "no violence," being of the opinion that the mere absence of swear words and blood would qualify the program as healthy Christian viewing for healthy Christian families.

BY WHAT STANDARD?

Too many Christian leaders have been following instead of leading. Instead of seeing biblical standards as higher ethics that rightly belong in a very high place, they see pragmatic relevance to today's culture as the moral territory they should occupy, and so they plant and replant their respective flags just shy of that receding boundary of "community" standards. Their line in the sand is redrawn daily to accommodate cultural "progression."

This shrinking territory of shifting sand is right next to the same place where cultural revolutionaries pull deviancy to even lower levels. Who would want to be straddling this border but the two-faced traitors who want to be accepted in the camp of the faithful and popular in the camp of the scoffer? It is no wonder that observers ask of Christian leaders, "whose side are you guys on, anyway?"

Some leaders are fond of reminding observers that Jesus himself would hang out with whores and thieves and tax collectors. They would be advised to read the accounts more closely. Jesus spoke the truth to outlaws, but he had no ongoing fellowship with covenant breakers. He never suffered fools gladly. Pharisees he condemned strongly. He was a champion of the very highest of moral requirements, even higher than the outward requirements of Mosaic Law.

It was repentant sinners whom Christ counted as His friends and, yes, He did spend a lot of time with repentant sinners of the lowest criminal class, to the consternation of men whose false righteousness had been elevated to an art form. Jesus loved these repentant sinners, and they loved Him back. The companions of Jesus were His sheep, whom He fed. He wasted none of His time entertaining self-righteous goats who loved a worldly diet.

In the last two decades, America has seen the development of a dangerously easy Christianity. Contemporary Christian music, contemporary Christian movies, and contemporary Christian church services perpetuate messages of an easy Christianity designed to be marketed to self-absorbed people who don't respond well to the tough messages of the Bible.

This contemporary methodology is oxymoronic. This new Christian message has to depart from the Bible in order to be marketable. I may be too young to see it, but I struggle to find anything that is Christian in this easy, man-centered Christianity which brands itself as an acceptably "cool" subculture that takes its cues from the world's culture but is still "Christian."

This must be addressed because there are many creative young Christians who intend to communicate "a message" through media. If these young Christians take their lead from a compromised and erring church, their lives' work will communicate error. As John MacArthur rightly observes, Satan isn't sowing the tares; church leaders are. Today's church leaders are also bending over backwards to accomodate the tares and keep them in the church so they can continue tithing and filling pews.

If young Christian media people think the trendy new leadership gimmicks hold creative clues for communicating with the world, and if they copy misguided sales-pitches, their productions will fail to have productive cultural influence.

Because error is off-limits to the Christian filmmaker, it's time to draw a bold line between so-called Christian filmmaking, which is cowardly filmmaking, and genuinely heroic filmmaking.

THE NATURE OF CHRONIC COWARDICE

For the purposes of this book, "cowardly Christian filmmaking" refers to projects, made by Evangelical

Christians, which communicate life-changing truth to a secular audience in a *hip, pragmatic fashion.* Typically, these projects fail culturally, spiritually, theologically, commercially, and artistically. There are several reasons for this, but the two greatest are a lack of knowledge and a lack of character on the part of the producer. Sometimes the producers can't see the life-changing truth or don't know the truth because they are spiritually infantile. Sometimes they know truth but are afraid to tell the truth as they see it. Sometimes the producers use pragmatic strategies to sell a message that is just as weak as the strategies are foolhardy.

But truth is never the servant of what works. From a structural standpoint, these projects fail because there is no hero in the story. The good news, which will be repeated several times in this book, is that audiences want to follow a real hero and his story. No hero, no strong box office returns. The good news is that returning strong heroes to our stories can help box office returns.

This audience preference is a fascinating remnant of Western civilization, lying deep in the souls of Western filmgoers, leftover from the strong Christian heritage that was once rich in every Western nation. That capital is almost all used up. Indeed, one of the few telltale remnants of a moral Western culture is this yearning on the part of movie audiences for the heroic, moral tradition. Because filmgoers communicate this (largely unconscious) preference with their spending habits, Hollywood sometimes reluctantly pays homage to this fact, usually when a suffering studio needs revenue. This is a rare occurrence, but when it does happen it is curiously ironic. Even in our decadent, postmodern culture, occasional Hollywood heroes are some of the last remaining reminders of a once-Christian society.

Now for the bad news. Very few Christian media people know what a hero is because they have been living in a religious church structure of chronic moral cowardice.

This is a strong indictment that must be acknowledged by aspiring Christian leaders, lest they repeat these mistakes. The modern Church culture is a stranger to historically militant, courageous Christianity. Since the mid-nineteenth century, the Church has descended into a compromised position of appeasement with the world and its values. This has been done primarily in the interest of winning souls, but the fruit of the compromise reveals spiritual failure and impotence. The Christian filmmaking effort is an illustration of this tragedy.

As script doctor Bart Gavigan says, movies are about values. The protagonist always reveals his own theology through the values he holds. There can be no such thing as a truthful Christian film without moral certainty in the hero. When Christian filmmakers follow the Church's "easy Christianity" script of theological compromise and easily moved values, they are lost. They don't know what to write, but it can't be heroism. Being followers instead of leaders, they copy the trends of a rebellious pop culture and fail in their calling and mission.

The last script I read by a serious Christian screenwriter was a particularly painful reminder of this. The basic story might have been a good one. The stated theme presented the truth that "forcing oneself into worldly conformity will not bring happiness." Which is not a bad theme, but it was actually very difficult to find that message anywhere in the script. Moreover, the treatment of the story made it clear that the writer either believed the lies of the Hollywood worldview or else felt he was beholden to perpetuate them. By Act II, he had paid homage to the following clichés:

- Businessmen are evil

- Small country towns are depraved
  because they are so traditional

- Work is to be avoided

- Sex makes the world go 'round

- Men are stupid

- Dads are dopey

- Fornication is inevitable after the "Hollywood kiss"

- License is virtuous

- Rebellion is inherently cool

- Selfish hedonism is a path to fulfillment and happiness

- Sin is an outdated concept

- Homosexuality is genetic and "gays" should
  be celebrated fixtures of society

- The State has a duty to provide a risk-free existence to its people

- Characters who curse are necessary as a mark of honest reality in a script

To be yet more graphic, the script included specific jokes that seemed to go out of their way to prove the writer's familiarity with Hollywood's idea of humor, including potty jokes, the newest sex slang, comparisons of Reagan to Hitler, racial minorities dealing out violent arrogance to white Anglo-Saxon males, and the mocking of a famous Christian businessman. A Bible-toting nutcase (actually labeled "Nutcase" in the script), totally irrelevant to the characters and story, made a cameo appearance for the sake of earning a PC brownie point. In the first few pages of the script the writer had already violated his own theme by forcing his script into conformity with the world.

What's going on here? Are all Christian scripts so comprehensively shaped by the Hollywood ethic? No, but the version of the script I reviewed was promptly optioned by an equally shortsighted Christian producer. Both writer and producer want to make themselves successful careers inside Hollywood and are trusting their "creative instincts" to conform to the politically correct culture. They have successfully conformed, and they may indeed succeed inside Hollywood.

This is an illustration of today's Christian pragmatism, which underlies today's chronic Christian cowardice. Weak message, plus confused presentation, plus celebration of worldliness, plus theological error, plus a blunt denial of God's wisdom and sovereignty, all rolled into one trendy package, is somehow supposed to do the hearer some good while entertaining him with shallow deceptions. As Christopher Catherwood has posed, "Try to replace sovereignty with savvy, and look at the results." Worldliness.

This is how the term "Christian filmmaking" has become pejorative. It's no wonder the world regards Christianity with contempt. Christians betray their King. Christians are ashamed of the essence of their Faith and sink even deeper into the moral confusion that is enslaving modern man.

Christ commanded all of us to examine the fruit. So what is the fruit of Christian pragmatism? The runaway worldliness of the Church is easily keeping pace with the runaway worldliness in surrounding culture. Christian radio, Christian television, and Christian movies have simultaneously descended to a level that is not merely culturally irrelevant, but spiritually treasonous. It is also ugly, childish, and of poor technical quality. This, of course, is a generalization, but it is an accurate generalization.

This fruit speaks for itself: Christian outreach has made itself culturally irrelevant.

Churches entertain but do not disciple, and so their spiritually impoverished families are dysfunctional.[76] Confused false converts misrepresent the church by identifying themselves with it, and most clergymen cannot defend the faith in the face of growing persecution. Psychotherapy has replaced biblical counseling, youth rebellion is epidemic, and church leaders respond by lowering the standard rather than raising it higher. This is a picture of moral cowardice.

THE HEROIC TRADITION

Can film do anything to fix this problem? Yes. It can teach the truth. It can recover one gift of Western civilization: the heroic protagonist. This figure, long a fixture of history and literature, must not be defeated by the modern cinematic anti-hero. The real and imagined heroes of literature, legend, and lore served to teach and inspire successive generations of barbaric people to turn from darkness to light, from barbarity to civility. Their determination to do this produced the character that fueled the development of civilization.

---

76. According to researcher George Barna, most U.S. pastors consider they are doing an excellent or good job in leading people spiritually. His further research contradicts this, revealing that: (1) Few congregants have a biblical worldview; (2) Half the people are not spiritually secure or developed; (3) Kids are fleeing the church in record numbers; (4) Most of the people who attend worship admit they do not connect with God; (5) The divorce rate among Christians is no different from that of the world; (6) Only two percent of pastors can identify God's vision for their ministry; (7) The average congregant spends more time watching television in one day than he spends in spiritual pursuits in one week.

Robert McKee, Hollywood's most influential scriptwriting tutor, reminds his students that true heroes are "the center of good."

The hero is not a guy who lowers his standards in order to be more comfortable. He's a resolutely normal fellow who, like all of us, faces moral tests. But he tries to conquer them. This is why people are willing to pay money to see the outcome in this dramatic challenge. The hero might fail, like we are failing. Or he might succeed, teaching and inspiring us as he does so. We know he is as weak as we are, but we want him to triumph over himself, over temptation, over the conflicts that tower in his path, and we want him to make the correct moral decision. The real hero settles for nothing less than triumph, and he triumphs in ways we don't expect him to.

Screenwriters cannot lower their own standards to be more acceptable while writing about uncompromising heros. We must stay true to biblical themes and ethics in order to teach and inspire.

Today's films need to reintroduce the concept of *character* to a dying civilization. Christians need to hear it and they need to appropriate character themselves. Then, by telling stories of character, they can disciple millions of moviegoers into heroic civility.

This is the way McKee puts it: "True character is only revealed in the actions of a character under pressure in his moral choices under pressure. The greater the pressure, the greater the revelation of character."

Three students of Robert McKee decided to apply what they had learned about the heroic tradition. They created motion picture blockbusters that resonated with a population starving for heroic examples.[77] But success stories like this must begin with the heroism of the writers and producers.

---

77. Peter Jackson, Fran Walsh, and Andrew Stanton, all former McKee "Story Seminar" students, earned a total of seven personal Oscars in 2004 alone. "Best Picture" (*The Lord of the Rings: The Return of the King,* Jackson and Walsh—Producers), "Best Animated Film" (*Finding Nemo,* Stanton—Writer/Director), "Best Adapted Screenplay" (Jackson and Walsh—Co-writers), "Best Song" (Fran Walsh—Co-writer), and "Best Director" (Peter Jackson). At the time of this writing, those two films have a combined gross of nearly $2 billion USD.

Chapter 7

VALIANT WRITING

The poet is in command of his fantasy, while it is exactly the mark of the neurotic that he is possessed by his fantasy. —*Lionel Trilling* [78]

Let's summarize the big lessons learned so far. Film is a fun vocation because it integrates so many challenging arts, sciences, technologies, and talented people. But it's more than entertaining fun. It is a religious weapon that has been used for both garish entertainment and subtle indoctrination. You need spiritual maturity in order to know how to use this versatile weapon because it teaches. Because every film teaches religious messages, you must understand the responsibilities you carry when you presume to use film to teach anything. You must have character as well as sound theological footing in order to rise to positions of responsibility in the industry. You must choose your positions and training carefully in order

---

78. From *The Liberal Imagination* (1950).

to avoid helping the wrong people advance the wrong ideas. You must develop the vision to be a leader and not a follower. You must attain to positions of influence in order to be the most effective teacher you can be. You must aspire to be an independent writer/producer/director.

The reason you want to be a writer is because writers choose and create the content of the messages that are ultimately seen on screen. The reason you want to be a producer is because the resourceful producer makes impossible productions a reality and chooses which messages are told. The reason you want to be a director is because the director brings the exertion of the producer and the wisdom of the writer to life, helping to craft these messages.

The project begins in the writer's domain with the creative idea that drives it. What will you write? What stories need to be told? How will they be told?

Your predominant medium as an influential filmmaker is the two-hour theatrical feature film. In the early twenty-first century, this motion picture format is still the influential pacesetter of American culture. As it is exported to other nations, it upsets cultural norms wherever it is seen. The "movie" moves the thinking and the worldview of entire societies. You will need to be familiar with the story structure of this two-hour format. You will need to know the grammar of the filmmaking craft. And you will need to have a comprehensive worldview of your own so that you do not perpetuate the errors of today's dominant religious worldviews of Marxist humanism.

First, take a look at the structure. Western audiences learn best from this format:

A flawed but sympathetic protagonist

summons moral courage to face and then overcome

increasingly difficult, seemingly insurmountable moral tests to achieve a compelling desire.

The best movies you've ever seen follow this structure. It's not a formula, it is form. This particular structure is brilliantly complimentary to the Christian worldview because the protagonist is a hero. This structure can illustrate the truth. It can teach moral authority. It can clarify ethics. It can elucidate the meaning of moral courage and can explain the applicability of biblical wisdom. It can show the world what masculinity is. It can show the beauty of manners and family life. It can tell the truth about evil and show the vast difference between bad character and good character. It can pit evil against good. It can criticize evil instead of good.

This is one reason the heroic tradition was so deliberately hijacked by neo-Marxists whose political strategy demanded cultural disintegration. Three generations of filmgoers have been confused about the nature of truth, courage, justice, and heroism. The films being created by confused filmmakers have cumulatively bad messages in them.

How much do you know about the heroic Christian worldview? Because it has been largely replaced by the statist worldview, it is not something you will pick up easily by going to a few Sunday school classes. The men who have best succeeded in mastering it took great pains with academic study, particularly in systematic theology.

Historian George Grant, of the King's Meadow Study Center, is an expert on early American history, and comments on the diligence of the American Founders to get their theology and worldview right, knowing that the ideas on which their new Republic was based would have long-lasting consequences. Writes Dr. Grant:

> This is precisely why the Founding Fathers made certain to ground their work toward building a great society of freedom and liberty on the unambiguous ideas of the Christian worldview. Throughout history that worldview had prompted the world's most remarkable flowering of art, music, literature, architecture, prosperity, and progress. For all its many failings, no other civilization had known the kind of justice, equality, independence, affluence, charity, development, compassion, beauty, advancement, mobility, and maturity as Christendom had. The American pioneers wanted to perpetuate—and perhaps even enhance—that legacy for the sake of their children, their children's children, and for all the succeeding generations that would come afterward. They were careful to avoid the errors of pagan worldviews which had, throughout the history of the world, continually unleashed the horrors of brutality, tyranny,

misery, and injustice.[79]

It is for precisely this reason that you must build your screenplays on the unambiguous ideas of the Christian worldview. The place to obtain a solid and courageous worldview is through the most solid and courageous literature you can find. Begin with the Bible. Find out what the Bible has to say about courage and true heroism. Then study books from the more heroic periods of world history. Look closely at the sixteenth through eighteenth centuries. Find out why the most courageous people of all time are people of faith. This is not mere opinion but a recognized fact even in Hollywood.

When a project needs a hero, he or she will be a person of profound faith, conviction, and moral courage. Hollywood merely places that hero's faith in something other than God. You may want to beware of Hollywood wanting to steal or borrow some of your ideas. Your stories may have the fresh, creative, and heroic angle Hollywood finds so hard to find.

Should you ever sell to Hollywood? Remember, even the most powerful Hollywood screenwriters have little influence over the final films based on their scripts. If a studio buys a script, they will generally assign a number of their staff writers to it to adapt it to a product more suited to the director the studio will choose without the writer's input. It is said in Hollywood that writers possess tremendous

79. George Grant, "Worldviews Matter," November, 6, 2003, *www.kingsmeadow.com.*

power... until they turn their scripts in. Every story is baptized into the neo-Marxist or humanist framework.

Another common gripe you should know about is that if a writer is unsatisfactory, the producers will hire a new one. If a writer *is* satisfactory, the producers will hire *five* new ones. This type of script-by-committee is becoming the norm for large-budget films. If one writer is good, ten must be better. Obviously, group brainstorming can be helpful, but to prevent your ideas from being stolen, changed, and retold, you should strive to be able to write, produce, and possibly direct your own films.

Spend a lot of time learning to write, outside of Hollywood. Then, try to keep your scripts outside of Hollywood. In Hollywood, writers are a dime a dozen. Some of them can actually write, and some of the resulting scripts follow the heroic structure well. This has led to an attitude that any decent writer can be assigned to a decent premise and he will write a good film. Along the way to the final edit, the project is inevitably defiled by the political gauntlet through which it passes. Our scripts must deserve better treatment. We should try to write truly great films, and we can, when our creative processes are guided by the right worldview and take shape creatively according to the character of the Author of life.

Christian screenwriter Brian Godawa explained this process in an interview with *Relevant* magazine. Godawa points out that screenwriters model our kind, loving, and providential God who designs the life-stories of all men, when they design all the elements of a fictional story. Filmgoers not only learn things from our storylines, they actually participate in viewing a story that was created in the same way God created his moral universe. God plans everything. Everything has a specific purpose, as it must in our films. Everything that happens in the movie's foreground, the background, and even in the music, is ordained by the writer. Everything that does not advance the character's story, the plot, and the theme is edited out in the creative process.

"So a determined universe is inescapable in the art of story," says Godawa. "Think of Romans Nine. Storytelling reflects the Christian God and His providential determination of the free acts of human beings. A screenwriter providentially creates characters based on the kind of story he or she desires to tell. Authors determine every single word, every single act, good and evil, of all their characters, down to the jot and tittle, sometimes working for hours on just the right turn of a phrase or subtle plot twist. Even events that seem like chance occurrences in a movie, like a freak car accident or the lucky throw of dice, are deliberately written in by authors to direct the story exactly where they want it to go. Yet when an audience watches the movie, we see characters freely acting and morally accountable for their actions in a world where some things appear to happen by chance. Our knowing that the characters and their stories are predestined by an author does not make them any less valuable or their stories any less meaningful. But this apparent free will and chance are shown by the end of the story to be parts of the ultimate self-revelation of the main characters and others—and that revelation was what the storyteller predestined in his orchestration of all the events. There is a plan to it all, even if the characters don't know it at the time. Thus storytelling reflects the ultimate storyteller of all history, God Himself. In this way the act of storytelling itself becomes an apologetic."

Although Godawa's recent films no longer reflect this principle, this statement is correct. The more a screenwriter learns about the character of God, the truths of the biblical worldview, and the truth of biblical storytelling, the more exciting his film production becomes.

CRAFTING THE SCRIPT

You would do well to read at least three screenwriting books in detail. Authors Robert McKee, Syd Field, John Truby, and Michael Hauge are probably available at your local library. There are perhaps nine hundred others available from major booksellers, some of which will tell you how to sell your scripts to the guys in Hollywood who will then change them. Don't sell your good stuff to Hollywood, and don't sell your bad stuff to them either.

After reading several books, you will realize that even screenwriting structure is more of an art than a science and that there are as many opinions on story structure as there are writers. But there are some general rules that undergird the craft. What follows is a very brief look at the kinds of rules with which you must make yourself familiar. The following opinions and overview are not meant to be exact instructions. If you can find McKee or Field, sit down and do the tutorial with them. They will go into much more detail about what follows. They will give you more precise guidelines and writing tools. They will describe the page format you should use, so you can then follow their comments about what should be happening in a certain script at a certain page. The properly formatted screenplay page, with slug-lines, dialogue, and subtext, properly formatted, represents about one minute of screen time, whether your film is a chick flick or a war drama.

Go ahead and spend the money on a scriptwriting, formatting software program. Movie Magic (*screenplay.com*) and Final Draft (*finaldraft.com*) are two of the more popular and intelligent programs. The software will free you from the restraints of having to be constantly concerned with format, allowing for greater creative freedom and experimentation.

But remember, these are only tools. So are the story structure suggestions. They are not a list of requirements that, if fulfilled, will automatically guarantee a good script. They will help you with the work, though. Particularly when your script isn't working. These tools will help you to analyze a script so that you can see what works and what doesn't and why. And, more importantly, how to change it so it does work. And an idea of structure will help you get started so that things work from the beginning.

Once you have your story in mind and your worldview flowing through your veins, there are basically two ways to write a script. The first is a sort of "stream of consciousness" writing, where you start at page one with a fuzzy idea of your characters and maybe a brief outline and let things develop from there. In this method, you may roll out two hundred pages. From those ideas, you try to mercilessly cut unnecessary scenes and characters until you're down to about 120 pages. In subsequent drafts, you analyze the structure to make sure it's as tight as possible. This is how most neophytes start writing, but a beginning writer will learn bad habits by trying this method first. I don't recommend it even for veteran writers.

The only real advantage to this type of writing is that things feel fairly fresh and spontaneous, the process is fun, and it generates a lot of other ideas. It has problems, though... without a clear picture of what needs to happen, a lot of dead scenes will be written, and the characters literally develop on the page, with no set back-story to drive them.[80] The haphazard construction makes it difficult to rewrite. Worse, the climax may be unexpected, so there won't be any dramatic foreshadowing earlier in the film.

The other method is known as the analytical approach, and is the one described in the better screenwriting books.

---

80. A character's back-story is the complete history of a character's life, including his worldview. There is no way to show every character's life story, but you, the writer, need to understand it thoroughly so you know how the character thinks and is likely to act in every circumstance.

The best architects build the best cathedrals, not the best stonemasons. The best analytical writers write the best scripts. By this method, you can write truly great scripts.

In this method, you would coordinate on paper every single element of your plot beforehand, so that every plot point and every turning point is meticulously matched to a scene specifically created for it. The script would not be started until a detailed plan is completely finished. The plan would include carefully comprehensive information.

Next, consider what genre is best for your story.[81] A Western, for example, does not need to take place in Dodge City in 1885. The popular, but theologically problematic film *Star Wars* was of the Western genre, even though it came in a sci-fi package with plenty of fantasy overtones and was very close to the Myth genre. The animated film *A Bug's Life* was also a Western (based loosely on *The Magnificent Seven*, itself a remake of Kurosawa's *Seven Samurai*).

Casablanca could have been a musical; it features twenty songs, more than most musicals. Instead, it was wisely crafted as a serious political thriller/romance. Films that can't quite decide what genre they are often don't succeed financially. Peter Jackson's *Frighteners* was part thriller, part horror, and largely comedy. Audiences found the comedy

---

81. The word "genre" comes from a French word meaning "kind, sort, or type." Typical film genres include Action-Adventure, Buddy, Cop, Black Comedy, Cinema Verite, Comedy, Detective, Disaster, Fantasy, Film Noir, Gangster, Slasher, Martial Arts, Romantic Comedy, Spy, Thriller, War, and Western, and sometimes combinations of the above.

too fanciful to take the horror too seriously, and the thriller too chilling to be able laugh at the comedy, and nervously gave it a pass.

Different genres of film have different requirements. Some have very specific requirements. A traditional murder mystery must have a dead body in the first act. A romantic comedy needs strong, realistic, endearing characters—the plot is important, but less so, and almost entirely affected by the characters themselves.

A heist film or spy thriller needs a big, complex, influential plot. The characters may not even be able affect the plot at all; they may merely react to its demands and cleverly accomplish their goals. In fact, if the plot is heavy enough, the character is usually developed purely to fit into the slots that the story requires.

Of course, great care must be taken that the audience doesn't realize that this is the case. Nothing should feel contrived or forced. The best way to ensure that this doesn't happen is to begin writing a film with a proper understanding of structure from the outset.

In your next step in building a script with the analytical method, your premise would be carefully crafted, answering the question, "what would happen if a hero like _____

tried to reach a goal of _____

but ran into _____

and was forced to choose _____

in his efforts to confront _____

because he really wanted _____?"

This helps you identify the facts about your hero. Whose story is it? Your hero is the one who really wants something badly and is having difficulty getting it. You would list your hero's outer motives and his major goal. You would list his outer conflicts and adversaries. You would describe his inner motives and flaws. You would deal with his inner conflict and self-revelation on paper and in a lot of detail. You would do the same thing with the hero's main adversary. You would examine the details of any romance or discovery.

Then write down an outline of every event that happens from beginning to end. Your plot will develop from this list. This is a great learning tool for a young scriptwriter. Armed with a book on film plotline, a first script written with this method is a good way to learn about all the tools for creating and moving a tight plot; inciting incidents, hooks, hangers, turning points, twists, act-breaks, and the other elements of script grammar. After building a plot from scratch while focusing only on the structure, the writer has a better understanding of how to recognize which plot points to use and when and where to put them.

If the plot is not coming together smoothly, ask these questions about your characters and story: Whose story is it? What does your hero want and how badly does he really want it? What does your hero need, whether he knows it or not? What's his greatest hope? His greatest fear? How should the audience feel at the end of the film? What should they have learned? What will the audience be rooting for? What things will make the audience feel tense or nervous? What is the tension in each sequence? How do each of the other characters help or hinder the hero in his quest? And most importantly, ask, *what is the ending?* Steven Spielberg has lamented that fact that too many writers don't have endings for their stories. The ending is everything. Spielberg is right; too many scripts are beginning, beginning, and beginning. There is no middle or end.

Sometimes it can help to write a film outline backwards: think of a strong climax and then assemble the elements that might lead up to it. After you've written several scripts, you'll find a method that joins the techniques of the pros with your own best talents.

And don't worry if there is a part of the craft you're slow about. Perhaps you're not very good at dialogue. No problem. There are plenty of professionals out there who specialize in certain aspects of "script doctoring." "Body and Fender" men help with the general structure. Dialogue experts help with dialogue. There were six different doctors brought in to touch-up the finished script for *Sister Act,* for example, most of whom were story structure doctors.

Script doctor Bart Gavigan says that "for every 15,000 writers who are good at dialogue, there is only one who is good at story structure." Gavigan stresses the importance of being diligent about learning the craft of structure because it is difficult, it is imperative, and it is indispensable for every script.

As your own method develops, you'll know how much time to devote to character development and plot development and which one to concentrate on first. They must contribute to each other and the story in general. This is difficult for a beginning author to achieve.

THE THREE-ACT STRUCTURE

In the 1970s, scriptwriter Syd Field was asked to teach a course on scriptwriting in Los Angeles. He didn't know what to teach. He began analyzing scripts to see if there were any recurrent forms and noticed a consistent organization similar to the three-act structure of plays. In 1984, he published his findings in a book, answering questions about the reasons feature films, seamless entertainment, are cut into separate pieces described by an archaic term.[82]

In doing so, he explained in simple detail what many successful screenwriters were doing without realizing it. The three-act structure is a useful organizational tool. It cuts a long script into small, manageable chunks: beginning,

---

82. D.W. Griffith pioneered the feature-length film, and projectors of the time required a film of that length to be on eight separate reels of film. In order to keep audiences seated while the reels were changed, directors created a cliffhanger moment at the end of each reel, and found that they could best divide the film into two reels for the first act, four for the second, and then two for the third act climax. To this day, three-act feature writers will often aim for eight strong climactic moments distributed roughly evenly throughout the film.

middle, and end. The most basic organizational concept delegates roughly twenty pages to Act I, fifty pages to Act II, and twenty pages to Act III, as you can see in the following diagram. A good writer will use acts to manage his plot points, the story arc, and his characters' growth.

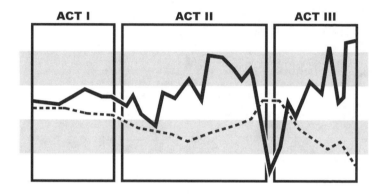

On this graph, the dotted line charts out the arc of an anti-hero. Many films today try to use this "out-of-balance" structure to create "realistic" stories of ineffectual characters. The plot meanders along with the protagonist's circumstances and then in Act III he ends up lower than before. This is depressing and boring. However, the solid line represents a good, strong character arc. The first act is exposition, not much conflict. In Act II, the fight begins and our hero is up and down, taking the audience on a rollercoaster ride of success and defeats, until the third act, where he recovers from some crushing blow and rises to victory.

Typically, the first act introduces the main characters, shows the audience a fascinating setting, and gets the plot rolling with an "inciting incident." During the course of the act, the subplot is laid out, the ingredients for the main plot are assembled, and then we have a little mini-adventure, perfectly set for the hero's triumph in the climactic third act. In Capra's *Mr. Smith Goes to Washington,* we find out about Jeff Smith. He's a humble disciple-maker. He works selflessly with young, disadvantaged boys to mold them into men. He doesn't want to be a big Senator, but accepts the call and shows us his heroic desire: he wants to honor the Founders, his father, and his family name by doing his duty well.

Act II introduces the complexities, risks, and tensions that fill out the drama and contains almost the entire story of the film. Here the hero is in for a rude shock as he is run up against the machinations of the villains. He's tested. His tests are often moral as well as circumstantial. If he's human, he stumbles or fails several times. This is so that he can succeed only by persevering and making the right, difficult moral choices. This is what makes him a hero. Let me repeat that because it's such an important definition. The hero is heroic because he chooses morality over moral compromise. This is real heroism. In *Mr. Smith Goes to Washington,* the inciting incident is moved into Act II. Smith writes an innocent piece of legislation that so happens to interfere with the plans of the villains, bringing their antagonism down on his head. The hero suffers cruel blows, but he passes the moral tests and does not compromise. At the end of Act II, he is shattered in defeat—a beaten man with packed bags, sneaking out of town, a disgrace to the family name and a failure in his calling. This is his lowest point.

In Act II, your hero's personal character becomes more open to the audience. We can see his inner struggles, failings, and his desires. Act II usually ends when things are looking darkest for our hero.

Act III begins when the hero hauls himself off the canvas one last time. In *Mr. Smith Goes to Washington*, Act III begins the following morning in the Senate Chamber during roll call. The name Jeff Smith is called and he responds with bold confidence, "Here!" The hero is up and fighting. He grits his teeth, and his actions must actively save the day in the film's climax. But just prior to the resolution of the film, there is usually a "twist." In *Mr. Smith Goes to Washington*, it appears that the heroic filibuster is buying enough time for Jeff Smith's young army of disciples to find out the truth and clear his name, confounding the villain in his grand scheme. Young boys battle seasoned hoods. The drama, conflict and tension, heat up in Act III to the boiling point. The "twist" comes when it appears that the villains win instead. The hero is spent; he has given his life and health in the fight. On the very verge of victory, his allies tell him the fight is lost and that he must admit defeat. The jagged line on our chart plunges, but only for a moment. The hero's very collapse is the incident that moves his antagonist, the senior Senator, to admit that the hero is right! The story is resolved in the climactic moment. Truth wins out, the hero's good name is restored, and the villain's cruel plan is stopped. The hero's arc finishes higher on the chart than ever.

Look at this structure again.

A flawed but sympathetic protagonist

summons moral courage to face and then overcome increasingly difficult, seemingly insurmountable moral tests

to achieve a compelling desire.

Now imagine that the first sentence is Act I, the next two are Act II, and the last line is Act III. The four events described define the story and what you must have in each of the acts.

There is no set length for each act, and different people have different opinions on how each should be measured. The most common view is that Act I is the first quarter of the film, Act II is the middle half, and Act III is the remaining quarter. This does make for a good pace for most scripts and stories. Director Barry Levinson believes each act should be of equal length, in terms of script pages, allowing the editor to time the acts out as needed. But others are more comfortable with the 30-50-20 page breakdown, keeping the pace of the climactic third act short and hot.

I personally believe that every story will have its own requirements. In fact, not all stories even fit into the very artificial three-act mold. *Raiders of the Lost Ark* is a seven-act film. This is a good example of the old adage; *artificial rules are there for you to break, but only if you know how to break them.*

Lawrence Kasdan was able to see the need for seven separate acts for Indiana Jones' adventure. Instead of trying to pack it into a three-act formula, he was able to give it the structure it needed. He also understood exactly how breaking away from the three-act mold could weaken his script, and he was able to compensate for that and in turn make an even stronger film. John Truby warns writers that the three-act structure can bog some stories down in unnecessary development in Act II, which is why Kasdan's ensemble western *Silverado* was developed as a four-act script.

CHARACTERS

Films need well-developed characters. The audience needs characters to empathize with and relate to. Film is a visual medium, so characters must be defined by what they do or say. This is both a limitation and a strength. We can't show thoughts as we can in written literature, but we can show clothing, body language, and *how* they do the things they do. This defines them.

But the characters need more than the understanding of the audience. They need the empathy of the audience. The beginning of the first *Rambo* film is a prime example of empathetic overkill. The writer pulled out every trick in the book and packed them into the first moments of the film because he knew he was working with a protagonist who was not all that likable: a mumbling, disturbed killing machine.

The film opens with Rambo hitchhiking, looking for an old friend of his. He finds the man's family and learns that his friend is dead. He experiences emotional heartache, and we ache with him. He gives his photo of the friend to the dead man's family. He shows that he is a kind man, and we like him for it. He gets back on the road, and is picked up by a local sheriff who takes him out of town and tells him to get lost. Our hero is being discriminated against, and we take it personally. Rambo refuses to leave the town, but turns around and walks back in. He shows perseverance and determination, and we applaud him for it. The local cops unjustly arrest him, and unjustly mistreat him, and we burn with righteous indignation! He escapes, fighting his way out, and we see that he is very good at what he does. We marvel at his skill and talent.

In under eight minutes, no less than *seventeen* different empathetic devices had been employed to manipulate the emotions and the empathy of the audience. This poor film probably succeeded at the box office because of a sound story structure.

The Rocketeer is a better film, and it's also a textbook example of simple script structure. Its weakest points have to do with the characters, but we should be able to learn from these.

The hero is Cliff Secord, a dashing young pilot in 1930s California. He and his pal Peevy are trying to build a new plane to fly in air races. They need the prize money. Through a few mishaps, we get to see Cliff's character. He's loyal, friendly, and a little hot-headed. Peevy is old, wise, and steady; Cliff's father figure. These are almost cookie-cutter characters. They don't have a whole lot of depth to them, and are weakly stereotypical.

A lot of Cliff's character exposition is provided by his girlfriend Jenny, some during the scenes with them together, and also, more effectively, when she describes him to a third person. This is a good technique; if all else fails and you simply must verbally communicate something positive about your hero, have a character close to him do it, in a painfully honest way.

Jenny is an aspiring movie actress, at the moment relegated to being an extra in crowd scenes. Nevertheless, she is still enraptured by Hollywood and the star system. Aha! Now we're getting something interesting. She's attracted to the actors in the films she works on, but is, maybe, in love with plain old crop-duster Cliff. He is scornful of her chances of becoming a star herself, but she likes the allure of Tinsel Town. Now we have some tension within her character and between both characters. Cliff doesn't like Tinsel Town. There's still not a lot of depth, but it's interesting.

It is very helpful to understand how to separate a character's main want and ultimate need. Jenny wants to be, and be with, a glamorous movie star, but she needs to learn that Cliff's a better bet for a husband (although mainly because he's the film's hero and the movie star is a Nazi spy). At the beginning of the film, the audience must understand exactly what she needs, and it's best if she doesn't have a clue. She is blind to understanding her real emotional *need*, and is too busy pursuing her more tangible *want*.

Up pops the villain to take advantage of this. Neville Sinclair is the glamorous star she dreams of, a well-loved, all-American hero of numerous swashbuckling action flicks. Secretly, he is also a Nazi spy. This duality within his character is also interesting, but never fully explained. When the villain learns Cliff has found the rocket-pack he has been trying to steal for the Nazis, he tricks Jenny to get more information from her.

Meanwhile, he has hired local mob boss Eddie Valentine to pursue Cliff. Eddie starts out as a caricature of a nightclub-owning '30s gangster, complete with wise-cracking henchmen, but when he learns that his employer is actually a Nazi agent, he rebels and stands shoulder to shoulder with the FBI, spraying Nazi Storm Troopers with his tommy-gun.

So in these last three characters, we see three different elements that make for interesting characters: internal tension, a contradictory dark secret, and a change of heart, respectively. The villain is the weakest of these, because we never truly understand his motivation, and more of his evilness comes from Timothy Dalton's great performance than from the story structure.

The story must make a distinction between mystery and confusion. The characters in this film are not well defined, and this is its first failing.

But even more important than definition and empathy is character growth. Your characters, especially your hero, must grow and finish the film more mature than he started. Here *The Rocketeer* fails again—for reasons relating to theme, to be discussed shortly. Cliff grows very little. During the course of the film, he realizes how much he cares for Jenny, and gallantly risks his life to save her, but he never truly grows.

Jenny does grow, however. Her experience with Sinclair's treachery leaves her far more mature and no longer starry-eyed. She finally understands her *need*, and adjusts her *want* accordingly. She is now more certain of her love for the now-heroic Cliff, and here we see another oft-quoted scriptwriting principle: *it is from the wound that the flower grows*. A character must have a weakness that needs strengthening, and the events of the film should cause that growth.

SYMBOLS AND MACGUFFINS

Film is a visual medium. It has visual limitations. It's difficult to show the mechanics of someone thinking or feeling.

Conflict has to be external to make it onto the screen, unless you want voice-overs, which are rarely effective. In order to show such things, you can use musical cues and lighting changes, but the best way to show internal motivation is to use symbolism, and the easiest way to do that is with a personal, physical object.

For example, in *The Patriot*, Mel Gibson melts down lead toy soldiers, a cherished possession of his dead son, to make bullets. Every time we see him pull a soldier out of his pouch, we know exactly what he is remembering. We don't need a flashback or a voice-over explaining his thoughts, we know that the soldiers remind him of his son's life and his son's death, and the bullets he is making symbolize the purpose of the fight, the resistance to a tyrannical enemy. A little heavy-handed, perhaps, but still a simple and effective symbol.

There's not a lot of symbolism in *The Rocketeer*. Jenny has a bracelet that Cliff bought her when he was a lowly crop-duster, but it is never used to show what she's thinking. It does, however, provide her with a good opportunity to explain and reflect on her feelings for Cliff. Like all good flying aces, he has the stock-standard sweetheart's-photo in his cockpit, which he risks life and limb to rescue after a crash. This shows his feelings well, but the photo does more to advance the plot when it is stolen by gangsters who use it to identify Jenny.

In this way, it is almost a MacGuffin. The MacGuffin is a plotting tool invented by Alfred Hitchcock. It is difficult to explain, because it can be anything—or nothing. It is whatever exists to move the characters to where they need to go and answer questions and give your audience something to focus on. Modern filmmakers often have a MacGuffin that is tied directly into the plot, whereas Hitchcock's were misdirection, hinted-at clues, or, sometimes, nothing.

Throughout the first half of *Psycho,* the audience is led to believe that the film is about the quest for a missing $40,000. That money is soon forgotten, and exists only to move the players in the story to the infamous hotel. In *North by Northwest* the MacGuffin has to do with what Cary Grant and James Mason's spy characters do. But Cary Grant isn't even a real spy, and we never learn what James Mason is, except for an "importer and exporter."

The film is a chase movie, and according to Hitchcock, the reasons behind the actual chase are not important—so long as the characters are real, and really being chased, and the story of the chase is strong enough to get the audience truly involved. This requires a very strong story and expert character handling. Most modern writers take the easy way out with MacGuffins that are more obvious and tied more directly into the plot.

The MacGuffin in *Star Wars*? The Death Star plans R2D2 secretly carries. It brings all the characters together and sends them on the adventure, but it also supplies them with the advantage to succeed in their quest. In *The Rocketeer*, it is, of course, the rocket-pack itself. It's a strong MacGuffin, but perhaps a little too strong. The goal of the MacGuffin is to get the plot where it needs to go without overstating the reasons for the MacGuffin to be there. It should never overshadow the story.

SETUPS AND FORESHADOWING

As said before, it's important that you, the author, know exactly what the plot is doing, so you can link the beginning and end of your script together with certain events. This is useful for getting the audience to remember what has happened before. However, the setups must be subtle, so the payoff is still unsuspected.

In the first scene of *The Rocketeer*, we are introduced to Cliff, the hero, and his sidekick as Peevy sticks a blob of chewing gum onto the tail of his new plane. This action stands on its own as a character development element, letting us see the relationship between the two, but it is actually a setup. Later in the film, a bullet punctures the fuel tank of the rocket-pack during a crucial action scene. There is no time to repair it properly, so the sidekick takes Cliff's gum and patches the leak.

It's a good payoff because it ties into the elements of the characters that we know, and references something that we've seen earlier. Also, it's a strong cliffhanger moment because our hero needs to use the rocket-pack *now* to chase the crooks and save the girl. However, this is, in itself, another setup! During the climactic face-off, Cliff is forced to hand the rocket pack over to the villain. There's a close-up of the bullet hole as Cliff slightly peels the gum away, just enough to allow some fuel to leak out.

As the Nazi jets off triumphantly, the rocket ignites the fuel leaking from the bullet hole, and our villain gets an explosive come-comeuppance. He gets justice, with a dose of irony. It is yet another strong payoff that ties into previous events of the film. It gives the audience a chance to see how the hero can be creative and innovative using something the audience knows just as well as the hero does. More importantly, though, its setup stands alone as a solid cinematic moment. There are no "hey, remember this for later" clues when Peevy patches the bullet hole that would suggest to an audience what would happen next and spoil the surprise.

This is a fine line; showing the viewers all the pieces of the puzzle, but doing so in a way that they don't put the puzzle together any faster than the hero does. But they *must* have the pieces; it's a weak climax where the hero suddenly reveals a skill or gadget that has never been mentioned before. It is equally weak when he picks up a stick of dynamite for no reason other than because he'll need to use it in the third act. Audiences notice these things.

The Rocketeer isn't finished with the chewing gum yet! In the peaceful final scene, Howard Hughes turns up to reward Cliff with a new plane to replace the one that was destroyed earlier. As he turns to leave, Howard tosses him a pack of gum, teasingly reminding him never to fly without it. This is also a reminder to us, the audience; it takes us back to the very first scene, and also both of the exciting plot points with the gum earlier. It's a strong bookend and a good close.

SUBPLOT

While we're on that scene, it represents a good example of a subplot. A good rule of thumb is that the main plot is resolved, and the subplot never is. In *The Rocketeer*, the main plot involves Cliff's attempts to rescue his girl from Nazi spies and win her back. The subplot is his desire to be a national air racing champion.

The main plot is simple, and hardly original. In fact, there are only a dozen or so main plots that will ever be used. I can think of hundreds of films with a "boy wins/ rescues girl" plot, most of which are very different from each other. If done correctly, the subplot is what makes the main plot interesting and unique; it should also seamlessly mesh with your characters and their growth.

For example, Cliff is a pilot who wants to be an air racer. This is the subplot, almost in its entirety. As we open in the film, he is flight-testing a new plane, which crashes. His hopes are dashed, but he finds the rocket-pack and plans on using it to make enough money to build a new plane. As a pilot, he is capable of flying the rocket-pack, which is convenient. However, the gangsters who shot his plane down are looking for the rocket, deduce that he's taken it, and kidnap his girl.

Now, the subplot events that have driven the main plot into existence are all major plot points, and the two are co-dependent and support each other. This is as it should be; they should strengthen each other and contribute equally to the strength of the film. But note that it is the main plot that is resolved; Cliff wins Jenny back, rescues her from the villains, who are either destroyed or redeemed, and fixes everything that went wrong.

Both Cliff's and Jenny's main character growth also comes from the main plot; Cliff realizes his love for Jenny, and she understands this and becomes more committed to him. All the main threads are tied up.

But the subplot is not. Cliff still has not realized his dream of being a racing pilot. Even though Howard Hughes turns up and gives him the new plane, similar to the one he lost in the first scene, that's all we see. As far as the subplot is concerned, he is right back where he started. And there the film ends and the credits roll. It's not important that we know whether or not he wins any races—it is mere subplot.

THEME

Now we come to the real heart of good screenwriting. Two excellent examples of scripts with strong themes are those for *Rain Man* and *The Verdict*. Neither of their structures are perfect, but both are good examples of careful handling of character arc and theme.

In *The Verdict*, the theme is truth, namely that the truth is important, even all-important, and worthy of professional and personal sacrifice to preserve. Everything in the script— every action and reaction—has to do with truth. Every obstacle in the film is the result of a lie, and every mystery revolves around finding out if a person is honest or if a statement is correct. Even the backstories of the characters revolve around truths and lies. In the end, the hero abandons the girl because he knows she is dishonest. This is a tricky ending to sell to an audience, but it works, partly on the strength of the characters themselves, but mostly because the theme is so powerful—if the audience understands the point of the film, they know our hero *can't* compromise anywhere. Associating with liars is just not an option.

In fact, the hero's own character growth is very simple; he just comes to realize what the theme of the film is, and in *The Verdict*, its simplicity is its strength. At the beginning of the film, our hero is a disreputable, opportunistic, pragmatic lawyer with no clients and a serious drinking problem (which is incidental to his character—the film doesn't dilute the theme by adding a temperance sermon). His journey is the ongoing discovery that truth is important. His redemption comes when this truth comes out and sets him free. He also follows the want/need dichotomy we discussed earlier; he *wants* to win a court case, he *needs* to tell the truth.

Rain Man's theme is one of brotherly love. Charlie Babbit childishly kidnaps Raymond, his severely autistic brother, in a desperate bid to contest the father's will and extort some payments for himself from the executor. Raymond loves Charlie, but his autism prevents him from showing it. Charlie loves his brother, but his immaturity prevents him from even realizing it. Nevertheless, when constantly torn between his own needs and those of his brother, Charlie repeatedly dies to himself to serve Raymond.

He does so begrudgingly at first, but gradually he becomes aware of the film's theme. When he does so, he experiences true character growth. He matures, and becomes more of a hero than an anti-hero. In fact, he grows so much that his desires change. His want (money) and his need (loving his brother) are different, and his new, Act III want is to live with his brother. This type of inconsistency could be a weakness to the story, but the script handles it well.

Charlie requires the money in order to keep his business running, but now he does not greedily desire it. Because of this understanding, the audience still wants him to get the money, thus fulfilling his first, main goal without compromising his newfound character. He then realizes his brother is better off in a clinic, and his love for him is so great that he lets him go back. The audience applauds his selflessness. This is a strong, universal theme, but even films with weaker themes can communicate good messages.

In *The Hustler*, Jackie Gleason plays an aging pool champ. The young Paul Newman is a better player, but he still can't defeat Gleason because Newman lacks the character, discipline, and self-mastery of the older man. When he obtains it later in the film, Gleason recognizes the fact that now Newman is unbeatable. It's a clear illustration on the importance of character, and how it is superior to skill in any important undertaking.

The film *City Hall* shows how mayor Al Pacino loses everything because of small compromises made early in his political career. This theme shows how small sins can't be covered up before they lead to large-scale ruin. This theme is apparent in *Mr. Smith Goes to Washington*, but Jimmy Stewart's battle against corruption more specifically shows why a good name is to be more desired than gold.

If films are true to their themes, they can be good films. Imagine how good a film could be if the theme, content, and theology were all accurate, consistent, and in agreement. Unfortunately, we now come to *The Rocketeer's* second great failing. It has no really good, powerful, unified theme. The themes it does have seem to be that Nazi baddies have no chance against the good, clean American spirit; swashbuckling '30s barnstormers are tough and resourceful; and puppy love conquers all.

These are comic-book themes that can make for an entertaining movie, but there is nothing particularly inspiring or unified here. The characters never have a great deal to do with any one of the themes, other than an "I love you" and "we can't let the bad guys win" sort of determination.

Raiders of the Lost Ark has a number of plot points in common with *The Rocketeer*, and it even has the same Nazi villains and a similar adventurous hero trying determinedly to foil them and save the girl. But it's a better film because it has a more specific theme. The antagonists are not merely undeveloped Nazi goons; they are Hitler's top agents, actually attempting to steal the awesome power of a real artifact with a real supernatural history. Indy tries valiantly to stop them, but in the end it is God's hand that strikes down the sacrilegious evildoers and protects Indy's life.

The theme is ultimately one of God's power and sovereignty, even if it is portrayed in a less than theologically-accurate way. Indy's character grows only when he realizes this. He goes from being a disrespectful mercenary scoffing at biblical truth as "hocus pocus," to a truly heroic warrior who understands God's authority and reproves his own employers for disregarding it. His character experiences true growth inspired by the film's righteous theme.

This must be the writer's goal.

SOUND STORY STRUCTURE IS NOT ENOUGH

The purpose of this chapter has been to demonstrate elements of successful story structure. It is not to endorse the above mentioned films or to imply that good story structure equals a morally righteous or theologically sound film. Films must be morally sound in both their structure and their execution.

What I've laid out in this chapter would be equally effective literary tools for Christian or non-Christian writers. Non-Christian authors will likely write some of the better books on story structure. Creating a well-planned story structure is easier, leaning on their professional experience, but that experience will not contribute to the truthfulness of your themes.

This is a double-edged sword, obviously. A good understanding of theme can be used to create edifying movies, or false, destructive ones. Most of the films mentioned in this book are weak at best.

Film allows a writer to completely create another world, one with "truths," values, and even physical laws which are diametrically different to those of reality. It is very simple to create a film-world based on a religiously secular humanistic worldview, one that accommodates a corrupt and evil theme.

The rules of scriptwriting will have a humanist's characters "growing" in response to the theme's "truth," but actually becoming more corrupt compared to God's truth. The better the structure of his script, the more convincing its message will be, as the framework accurately reflects the logical cause-and-effect of reality but none of its moral laws.

But this is wrong. A believer's films must be morally responsible as to their structure, their themes, and their execution. Our themes must reflect a comprehensive Christian worldview based on God's truth. They must reinforce virtues that may be very unpopular at the moment.

For example, self-discipline, compassion, responsibility, friendship, work, courage, perseverance, honesty, loyalty, and faith. Most of these ideas have been demeaned in film and popular culture, but they are the building blocks of a strong theme.

Sometimes non-Christian writers draw from these themes in creating the premises for their films. The humanistic worldview is self-destructive and non-sustainable, and rarely interests audience looking for a cohesive, strong story.

At the 2004 Screenwriting Expo in Los Angeles, I attended a presentation by screenwriter and UCLA lecturer Jack Epps Jr, who explained to the groans and boos of his Hollywood audience that because America is a Christian nation, films must reflect some "Judeo-Christian storytelling traditions" in order to reach a large American audience.

He went on to describe how many of the producers and directors of his own films often rejected his story points in order to change villains into main characters and turn morality into a joke. In his opinion, this is the reason that several of the big-budget films he wrote, in particular *Dick Tracy*, were failures, dramatically and financially. Wiser filmmakers often borrow Christian values for greater success.

On example the Robert Zemeckis film *Back to the Future*. Biff's life of evil in 1955 is turned upside down when weak George McFly is inspired by his son's courageous influence. A leap back into the future shows that Biff is no longer a tyrannical bully—he's learned his lesson. In fact,

George McFly's entire family is blessed by the fruit of moral character when George summons moral courage. The story illustrates multi-generational results of a heroic conviction, though it presents the story in the context of many attitudes which are distinctively pagan.

In the second film, we see an alternate version of the future; one in which Biff is given nearly unlimited wealth and influence. In thirty years, he is shown to have completely destroyed his world, filling it with bars, porno theaters, pawn shops, and casinos. He owns the police and gangs run riot in the streets. It's a hellish example of how the people groan when evil men rule. We then jump back in time to get better insight into how his corrupt past led to a worse future.

This becomes even more apparent in *Back to the Future III*, where we see the patriarch of Biff's family, the murdering, stagecoach-robbing desperado, "Mad Dog" Tannen. It is obvious that if unchecked, the lawlessness in this family carries through to its descendants, influencing their culture. The audience understands this instantly, whether they believe that the sins of the fathers are visited upon their sons or not. They may not even believe in the concept of sin, but the film clearly shows that sin is both evil and destructive, and must be defeated by righteousness.

This is the power of film. Film communicates ideals even better than it communicates ideas. The Soviet propaganda films did not feature long discourses on academic Marxist theory; they showed characters suffering at the hands of non-Marxists and then aided and redeemed by Marxism. False themes as reality can be presented very convincingly as a shadow of truth, but film becomes most powerful when it communicates God's truth.

Unfortunately, as in the case of *Back to the Future*, to bring the film to a basically righteous conclusion dealing with redemption and generational faithfulness, the audience is bathed in numerous unchristian elements which taint the power of the message and communicate mixed signals. If our goal were simply to make films which are "more moral" than the typical Hollywood film, we would be satisfied with the results of *Back to the Future*, but the vision of the Christian filmmaker is much higher than this. Our goal is to glorify God by making films that are presuppositionally biblical in their structure, their themes, and their execution.

Chapter 8

RESOURCEFUL PRODUCING

Many calculations, victory; few calculations, no victory.
By means of calculations I can behold victory or defeat.
—Sun Tsu

Sun Tsu, the ancient Chinese general still regarded as a definitive military strategist, wrote that strategic warfare leads to victory. This book has outlined a basic strategy for finding victory in the media war. The basic formula: art, plus science, plus skill, plus character, plus spiritual maturity, plus independence, is a winning strategy. Can you pull all of these together in the making of a film?

Each element compliments the other. None can be compromised without leading to temporary defeat. Some talented young filmmakers have compromised their *independence* and have experienced long-term defeat. They broke into the industry, but became lifelong indentured servants in the process. Independence is the element that will allow you to be the leader you were meant to be without compromising the integrity of your messages.

Shortly after I had discovered the power of computer animation, I became inseparable from the computer. Every day I could try a new filmic technique. By the time, I was fifteen and I had a solid reputation because I was working with adults in the industry who liked my discoveries and were impressed with my work.

I enjoyed the reputation almost as much as I enjoyed the thrill of being able to create the impossible on the screen. I loved the power of being a one-man filmmaker. I loved animating. I could make the computer create something that existed only in my imagination. I could have been happy doing this, I thought, forever.

My dad kept an eye on this and made a steady effort to keep my feet on the ground and my vision on priorities. Many times, he would lean over my shoulder and quietly remind me that I was not being trained to serve as a pawn to advance the agenda of those filmmakers who are at war with God and His kingdom. In fact, I was not being raised to be a pawn at all, but a leader. To be a leader, I had to attain the skills which would ultimately allow me to lead projects. I had to pay my dues and acquire the skills which would allow me to someday attain independence as a writer/producer/director.

Thank God for a father who took time to shepherd me. I needed to hear this counsel and receive these admonitions.

I still benefit from such reminders and remain grateful for a father determined to help shape in my life the character and vision necessary to become a leader for the glory of God.

In the final analysis, it is the leaders who have the independence to shape culture for good or for evil. Employers, not employees, steer the content of the production. Employees in the animation departments certainly don't. Many film employees don't mind being employees because they're so thrilled to be on the project doing *anything*. And film crews do have great fun; almost every job related to film is fun. But no matter how good you may be as a DP, a costume designer, or visual effects supervisor, remember: *the true warrior sets his sights on being an officer.*

To be a chief you must first be an indian. All great future leaders begin as servants. Through service you acquire the knowledge and skill to become a leader. Of course, the more you know about each profession in the industry, the more qualified you will be to become a chief. If you serve as an apprentice or employee, serve with integrity and learn all you can as fast as you can. You're moving toward independence. Keep moving toward it.

But think twice before you sign-on to make a rival, unworthy chief victorious in his corrupt objectives. This is defeating the overall purpose of following your true Commander-in-Chief—the Lord Jesus Christ—to attain overall victory in the multi-generational, cross-cultural media wars.

The way to maintain professional independence throughout your entire career is simple: keep the overall goal in mind. Place yourself around worthy men. Serve great leaders. Choose the best projects. Make your leaders and their righteous projects successful. Serve that good leader well and watch yourself become more skilled and professional every day. Service is the incubator of true leadership.

However, if you can work on small productions of your own, you are learning to lead and learning to produce by actually leading and producing. You are learning to assume responsibility for every aspect of the production. You are asserting your independence by directing your own productions, gaining the experience and faithfulness necessary to produce really big productions.

Even though this is the hardest route to success, I endorse this approach for several reasons. If you can produce your own projects, you are learning first-hand about every job in the industry, including the business aspects of entrepreneurial filmmaking and the demanding rigors of professional tenacity.

If your goal is to be a filmmaker, you do need to achieve the status of writer/producer/director. Making films, big or small, is hard work. There are thousands of things that can go wrong and will go wrong. If you don't have the entrepreneurial ability to breathe life into a project and the tenacity to see it through, you won't be a real filmmaker, no matter how talented you are with the arts and sciences of the craft. Even the smallest video production project will force you to discipline yourself to overcome each hurdle with professionalism.

If you're working from home, you can involve your family in your projects in ways that benefit your family and benefit your own character development. I emphasize this because home is an environment that is too easily dismissed by aspiring professionals as a hindrance to their goals and plans. The virtues one gains from living in the tough, day-to-day rub of intimate and sometimes frustrating family relationships can provide the very character the professional is so desperate to attain for his life's work.

If you are like many aspiring young filmmakers, you have some production gear at home. (If you don't, see Appendix B.) You may have enough to attain true financial independence from which you can launch bigger and more important productions. In creating small family productions, your family members can be invaluable as sources of creative ideas, client ideas, project ideas, program ideas, script ideas, occasional sales, and even as cast and crew for your shoots. If you have younger brothers and sisters, teach them what you're learning. They can also be your best critics, helping you to evaluate your work from an honest perspective. What sorts of projects can you do with your family?

THE HOW-TO DVD

There may be numerous small-to-medium enterprises in your area which would pay for a DVD or VHS video that they can duplicate for distribution to potential clients. Larger corporations may pay five to ten times more if the concept and production values are superior.

Small business owners are the heroes of today's economy. If you get a creative idea about ways you could improve someone's business with special DVD content, tell them your idea. Look through the yellow pages for companies and services that suggest a how-to video.

Listen to conversations; what do people want to know? How to sell my own books on Amazon.com? How to make money on eBay? How to get out of debt? Maybe even how to make a how-to video? Bill Meyers has built a business almost solely on that last suggestion, and sells DVDs explaining how to make a how-to video over the Internet.

THE TELEVISION COMMERCIAL

Companies who advertise may pay you to create a single ad or an ad campaign for their company. These are traditionally produced by the television station as part of the price the advertiser pays for the advertising time. For larger ad campaigns, an ad agency will create the ad concept, hire a production company to create the commercials, and buy the time on several targeted stations. As soon as you know the capabilities of your equipment, pitch the most creative ideas you can confidently produce.

There is no reason why you could not eventually begin offering the services the ad agency offers. Companies pay agencies because the companies don't know how to represent themselves to their potential or existing customers. They want the agencies to tell them. If *you* can tell them and produce the media they need, you could pitch an entire package to any company you have the courage to approach.

THE WEDDING VIDEO

To be consistent with my thesis, I must admit that any production you undertake will improve your abilities as a writer/producer/director. Even wedding videos. I've shied away from these for several reasons. Profit is hard to come by except in very high-end wedding events. To make a local wedding video business prosperous, one would need to make it an exclusive pursuit, which may be fine for a season. An exclusive pursuit may distract you from better opportunities. Not a good choice for short-term video production.

THE GOVERNMENT VIDEO

With the exception of one emergency military project on a defensive weapon system, I've stayed away from these for a number of reasons of principle. Most government videos exist to expand the domain of the government to justify larger departmental budgets. The wasting of confiscated tax dollars is wrong, even if the waste goes into your bank account for a job well done. Additionally, government contracts can take years to finalize and years to quantify as being completed. Not a good choice for short-term video production, as tempting as the large contracts may be.

PUBLIC AFFAIRS DOCUMENTARIES

This is a market you should be involved in even if you're a successful movie mogul. Until you are, it may be the best market to tap in order to hone your skills and earn production dollars. A public affairs documentary is an analytical news editorial that uses narrative, exclusive interviews, graphics, and music to inform targeted audiences. They should be research-intensive. Public-affairs and political documentaries have been produced primarily by television networks since the early days of television. Most were as biased as the network management, which was usually... a lot.

Because these were so expensive to produce prior to the mid-1980s, very few independent documentaries were made for large audiences. One exception was in 1958. The Xerox Corporation agreed to sponsor an independent documentary on Soviet space efforts. When the networks refused to air the David Wolper production, Wolper personally contacted 150 television stations that agreed to air the program independently. In 1982, businessman John Hendricks launched a cable channel dedicated exclusively to documentary programming. Today, The Discovery Channel boasts nearly a billion subscribers worldwide, and numerous spin-off channels.

Documentaries such as the vehemently inaccurate *Fahrenheit 9/11* can bypass broadcast and cable outlets entirely by going into theaters or onto the Internet. Many half-hour documentaries have been made for the direct-to-video market for a lot less than the estimated $6.5 million Michael Moore spent on *Fahrenheit,* or the alleged $8.5 million Ken Burns spent on his Civil War series, which aired on public television stations.

With the proliferation of VCR machines in the late '80s, independent docos could be distributed directly to homes. Political candidates also experimented with "parlor videos," seven to twenty minute stump-speeches or biographical sketches of candidates, shown by supporters to neighbors. Long-form documentaries were distributed by churches, large ministries, and think-tanks to tens of thousands of households. Independent producers learned to set up their own distribution warehouses, going on talk-radio to promote their latest releases of independent journalism. Many of these independent productions were cablecast on local outlets by fans who simply took VHS copies of the production to the local studio and demanded a free time slot.[83]

---

83. Pursuant to Section 611 of the Communications Act, local franchising authorities may require cable operators to set aside channels for public, educational, or governmental ("PEG") use. Public access channels are available for use by the general public. They are usually administered either by the cable operator or by a third party designated by the franchising authority. Local residents can request studio facilities, playback facilities and broadcast time for programs that do not violate FCC standards of decency.

As long as the dominant media is biased toward the left, there will be a market for right and center-right documentaries that explain issues honestly and fairly. Exercise some entrepreneurial creativity; you'll need it when you're attempting bigger productions later. Start with small documentaries. If there are issues you would like to research and explain, you might find a sympathetic think-tank that would agree to purchase a few thousand copies from you, or they might pay to produce a program they would own. During election years, the independent documentary may be one of the best independent means by which to explain complex controversial issues to households. Special-interest groups might pay you to produce these. Some cablecasters might also pay you in advance to create a program, or might buy the rights to air a completed program.

For your first documentary, choose a topic that has a ready audience. Make sure you will be able to sell at least two hundred units. If your topic is this "hot" in terms of broad interest, approach organizations that may wish to co-produce (help you pay for it), buy it, or own it. Also, approach broadcasters and cablecasters. If no one wants to risk financial assistance, and you still think you can sell the finished product, make sure you have a means by which you can sell it. Fulfillment houses can warehouse your product, take calls on their toll-free telemarketing lines, fulfill your orders, and send you perhaps 75-80 percent of what they take in. Negotiate carefully with any fulfillment house. Insist on weekly accounting and payment schedules.

A typical retail price for a half-hour VHS documentary is $19.95. A think-tank might buy it from you for between $6.00 and $12.00 and give it away as a gift to donors who donate $25.00 or more. DVD prices change by the season, so shop around if that is going to be your final format.

Count the costs of production. Budget carefully. Stick to your budget during production. Evaluate your ability to advertise the product. It's still a risk, but is it a manageable risk? There are many stories waiting to be told about world history, American history, forgotten history, economic issues, bureaucratic issues, complex financial issues, medical issues, bogus legislation, education, whistleblowers' stories, science, the family, media, foreign policy, academic issues, the United Nations, military issues, basic constitutional issues, and more general issues of faith and personal liberty. Positive stories can be told in an uplifting way, and negative exposés can be conducted judiciously, unlike Michael Moore's poison-pen hack jobs.

You do not need to be a trained journalist to write and produce a documentary. If you are honest with the facts, defame no one, and are sure you can defend every statement in a court of law, you will be able to create documentaries of high credibility. Study truly well-made documentaries and don't get caught imitating current trends sparked by one-hit-wonders.

THE FOUR-MINUTE TELEVISION FEATURE

As more television channels go to air, the celebrity television talent pool loses its commanding presence. Viewers are no as longer loyal to popular TV faces and talking heads. They channel-surf. They tend to land on channels or programs that give them what they can't get on the radio and Internet: in-depth analysis or "human interest" stories. This is an opportunity for you to earn experience and dollars as a freelance writer/producer/director. If you're a wise Christian, you may be able to compete very favorably in creating stories that challenge the mind and touch the heart.

CBS president Andrew Heyward is not the only television executive who believes this is the future of prime time television, and is committing resources to it. Broadcast and cable stations pay the most for independent features that air in prime time. This opens an opportunity for you to create superior freelance stories for news outlets, television magazines, and specialty cable channels. There are outlets that will pay you for good visual storytelling. If you learn to tell stories well in commercials or in 3-7 minute specials, you will be much better positioned to storyboard and edit your first feature.

The most proficient visual storytellers are television press photographers who cover the news and short news features. Most work with producers or reporters. But many of them simply receive a call from an editor to go out and get a story on their own. They must make sense of the story visually, capture everything they need to tell the story, come back to the station, and edit the story all in less than a day. So, en route to the story, their visual storytelling skills are being exercised. How much time do they have? How much footage can they shoot? Sometimes they have only minutes at the news site and must budget their shots carefully. The less footage gathered, the simpler the edit session. What are the priority shots to record? How can they streamline the number of shots to tell the story fully but not bog down the edit process? These demanding conditions force them to think efficiently and visually.

These photo-journalists have learned to see the visual elements of stories. They've learned to know what elements flow into others. They've learned to frame the entire story by carving it up mentally into small pictures, which they grab efficiently and edit very quickly.

These guys are real professionals. Unfortunately, too many of them are equally clever at repackaging the truth into politically correct lies. Every day. With professional efficiency.

Could you do what they do as a freelancer? Packaging the truth with journalistic integrity? Phone the news editors in your area and see how much they'll pay you for freelance news or human-interest stories. Many of them will gladly pay you for your material if it is of superior quality, and they may phone you with the plum jobs. The skills you learn in doing this will strengthen your producing skills.

The freelance news story may be only a minute long, and such assignments would be rare. It will be more likely that you could sell the four-minute feature, typically a "human interest" story. The journalist who defined this genre was the late Charles Kuralt, who went to work for a local newspaper immediately on graduation from college. He asked the paper if he could write columns about real local personalities, particularly the "little guy." Kuralt's warm, intimate portraits were an immediate hit with readers and were later published in book form.[84]

Then CBS television asked Kuralt to do something similar with the "On the Road" series which Kuralt hosted for many years, deliberately driving with his two-man crew onto America's most obscure back roads, looking for good stories about salt-of-the-earth Americans. Kuralt simply told stories. Many of them were family stories. You may be surrounded by stories in your communities that are just as good.

What local stories could you find that would be worth telling well and telling accurately? There is a market for well-crafted stories about faith, family, freedom, entrepreneurial struggles, and community drama. Think about the stories you would like to see on the screen and go out and tell them in the way you know they need to be told.

---

84. Kuralt's visual writing style was apparent at a young age. Readers may wish to study his portraits in the book *Charles Kuralt's America*, Anchor Press, 1996.

THE SHORT FILM

The first and most important thing to know is that short films do not make money. At least for now, and even in the foreseeable future. They only really serve two purposes: as a learning ground for skills directing and writing feature films, and as a demonstration that you've learned these skills.

The short film is most valuable for directors who are trying to move into feature work. There is a slowly increasing market for shorts, though. As short film festivals grow in popularity and influence, there may be more interest in DVD compilations of award-winning shorts. Television or cable channels sometimes play short films as fillers, as do airlines. All of these outlets will pay small licensing fees, but the huge number of available shorts and limited demand prevents it from being a large sum. Internet distributors also allow you to make a small amount of money, and if you manage to create a very popular short very cheaply, you might make your budget back.

But unless you win a large cash prize at an A-list film festival, you are unlikely to turn a profit. Even professionally made and fully-funded films such as BMW's *The Hire* series or Reebok's *Terry Tate: Office Linebacker* shorts have only served as advertisements that may never make back their initial investments in anything other than brand identity awareness.

A large number of the "high-profile" short films are created with funding from tax-supported film commissions, by directors who are hoping to win awards from highbrow festivals in order to get respect from the movers and shakers in Hollywood. These shorts generally feature pretentious and depressing storylines with dysfunctional or rebellious characters. The filmmakers believe this is the requirement to be taken seriously by Hollywood, because they know how Hollywood thinks. They are right. The non-commercial system of festival showings usually means that these films have R- or X-rated "realism" as a further demonstration of their unfettered, nonconformist creativity.

But the short film as a director's tool is very valuable to us as well. Despite its somewhat tarnished reputation and inability to be a sure financial investment, creating a good short film with a solid story is a good exercise. A well-made short needs a beginning, middle, and end. Telling a three-act story in 2-15 minutes can take more skill than to do so in a feature-length film.

Directing a dramatic short with dialogue is probably the only way you will get experience trying to get real performance from actors, similar to what you will need to do with a real feature. But feature directors have weeks or months to develop relationships with their actors and learn how to motivate them, whereas short films may be shot over three or four days, making it a big challenge.

Experienced directors and professional producers understand the limitations and strengths of the short film, and will be able to see the expertise and worldview of the writer and director of the final product. You shouldn't fall into the trap of using short films to get work in Hollywood, thus become assimilated into its culture; but they are a useful tool for learning the craft, and for demonstrating what you have learned to independent investors.

There are eight basic types of short film, and you should be familiar with all of them:

Parody or Homage: A spoof, like *George Lucas in Love*. If you are going to parody something, pick something well-known, and do so creatively, without getting sued. Try mixing two unobvious sources.

Adapted Works: A film based on some other work, such as a song or short story. It is imperative that you are able to get the rights so that you are able to show and potential to sell your final product.

Mockumentary: An obviously fictional documentary purporting to be a true account of outrageous circumstances.

Personality-Inspired: A short that is based on a particular personality of an actor that you have access to. *InsideOut* was partly inspired by the lead actor's skill as a mime artist.

Gag: A simple short with a simple story and very little character development. Usually dialog-free, just an intriguing situation with a punch-line for a humorous ending. Essentially a joke... or a one-panel comic strip.

Skill-Inspired Demo Pieces: A piece that specifically shows off a skill that the crew might have. For example, directors who can create effects or are trying to develop a reputation for working with effects will have lots of dinosaurs and/or spaceships.

New Devices Based: Something specifically aimed at the Internet or cell-phone markets; something visually simple with no dialogue or subtitles and suitable for downloading onto a small screen.[85]

Wannabe Features: The most popular among film-school graduates looking for their first feature. A complicated short film with plenty of dialogue and plot that is trying to feel like a feature, or a scene or two from a feature.

Once you've made two or three short films, you will have a pretty good idea of how to make a feature. If you've done a good job, and made a good short, it will be obvious to professionals that you've mastered the production process and are ready for feature work. If your goal is to use the short to sell yourself and your story idea to a distributor, make sure that you can do so as a co-production, maintaining all the control possible over your script.

Make sure your short is backed up by a script you want to make as a feature, and that you already have some interest from a producer, and possibly an actor as well. If you, as

---

85. For more information about using the internet to distribute short films and changing rules of viral media, I recommend *The Future of Web Video* by Scott Kirstner.

the director, have a writer and producer, complete with a
finished feature script and a professionally made short film,
you already have extra bargaining points. The more interest
that you can generate from different parties the better.
If you can get your own producer *and* a reasonably large
investment as an independent, you might be well placed
to negotiate a co-production contract with a distributor
that allows you *full* creative control. Yes, this can happen
outside of Hollywood, and will happen more often as more
independent production dollars become available.

ACCOMPLISHING A WORTHY LIFE'S WORK

Will you make it as a filmmaker? Will you ever get to do
what you were really meant to do or will your name only
appear on the credits of a few mediocre films that deserve to
be forgotten a month after they come out?

If you've come this far in this book, you will have a
vision for assaulting today's corrupt media dominance with
truthful productions. You will want to replace the dominion
of a corrupt cartel with real leadership. You will want to
make productions that are significant enough to give you
lasting influence. Your productions will have to have enough
"punch" in the content to have the kind of wide-ranging
influence you what them to have. What are your messages?
What are your big projects that are worthy of big audiences?

Theatrical feature films still drive the worldview trends
of a culture. Keep an ongoing file of feature treatments you
would someday like to produce. Television will maintain

the worldview trends through entertainment programming, news, human interest, and public affairs programming. Keep a file of short-feature and documentary programming you would like to do.

As your list grows, you'll become wiser in your choice of material, in your storytelling ability, and in your ability to assess projects. As you study your growing list, you will know how much money you will need to do any one of your favorite projects. Big ones will cost millions. And you might run into people who tell you, "sacrifice some of your independence and we'll give you the money to make that project. With a few changes, of course."

When money comes along, will you be able to stand your ground and hang onto your independence, your integrity, and the integrity of your project?

If there are any strings attached, you won't have independence. Be sure you make distinctions between strings and genuine improvements. If your backers have suggestions on which there can be mutual agreement ahead of time, then you are not surrendering but receiving a blessing. Every string is a compromise of your independence, but wise advice from a financial ally may be a providential gift that strengthens the integrity of your project. If you are wise and humble, you can accept this gracefully and graciously.

So how can you strengthen your resolve and hang onto your independence? Build your independence on wisdom.

Develop your wisdom by producing and creating small productions that have integrity.

Stay busy with these independent projects. While you work on them, perfect your character, expand your skills, and enlarge your bank account by selling productions suitable for small audiences. Invest your profits slowly into bigger and bigger productions. Don't be timid about starting small. And pack-out your file cabinets with outlines, scripts, and treatments for worthy films.

THE ANATOMY OF A WORTHY PROJECT

What kinds of projects should go into your file cabinets? The first answer is this: Only work on those projects which are pleasing to God. A project should be more than "moral," in the general sense of the term, it must be biblical in its worldview, goals, and execution. I recognize, of course, that just as there are no perfect churches and perfect families, there are no perfect film projects. This being said, projects must be evaluated for their basic worldview commitments and there is a threshold at which a film project can be described as distinctively pagan, or distinctively Christian.

In the context of working on Christ-honoring projects, begin by collecting worthy stories with clever premises. Simple ideas with universal but righteous appeal are perfect. Make sure the subject is presentable in a way the audience has never seen it. Make sure the theme is universally recognizable and the message morally challenging. In the case of a narrative, make sure the hero is genuinely heroic.

Be sure the story offers the opportunity for strong but subtle worldview development. Then improve your story with collaborative development. Collaborate with your family.

Make sure the story structure involves a morally triumphant hero, believable moral tests, and clear moral distinctions. Write your story into a four-page treatment. If family and friends think it's worthy of being filmed, go to work on the script. Even before the script is finished, you could be working on gathering your production budget.

FUNDING

One of the producer's biggest jobs is getting the money and managing the funds. If you are completely independent, you will be using your own funds in the production of your film. If you have friends who wish to invest with you and share the profits, allow them to participate, but don't give them too much creative control if they would be unwise storytellers. If you're involving other investors, you have a fiduciary responsibility to them to manage every penny carefully and to be a good steward of their capital investment. Show them a business plan that outlines the marketing effort is as much detail as the production plan.

The business plan must also inform them honestly of the high level of risk involved. Films are risky. In many cases, every penny is lost as well as the time the filmmakers invested in the project. If you have some small productions under your belt, you'll know just how many things can conspire against a production and plan accordingly. This is why you would be wise to keep your project low-budget, and work with friends who are willing to take a gamble on you.

Chapter 9

PROFESSIONAL DIRECTING

What can happen is that you can get too used to having the money solve your creative problems, and the nice thing about doing a low budget movie is that you're forced to be creative all the time.   —Robert Rodriguez

During a production, the director is the responsible agent for creating a finished film. He does far more than rehearsing the actors and saying "action" on the set. He must interpret the script artistically and morally. He must choose the design of the entire production, selecting perhaps hundreds or thousands of elements that will make his overall vision a reality on the screen.

These elements include the actors hired to act. They include each of the professionals hired who will help him craft the "look" and "feel" of the picture. The director makes choices of professionals based in large measure on his knowledge of their past work, but also his knowledge of the arts and sciences of filmmaking.

Because lighting is so critical to the mood of each scene, many directors design their own lighting, hiring a head gaffer to supervise the technical side of bringing in the right lights, stands, gels, power, and cables for the job. Lighting specialists and grips are some of the most resourceful people on any movie set. The grips assist in the placing of the camera and any dollies or cranes used to achieve a certain shot.

The director must also hire the cinematographer best suited to handle any unique lighting conditions the director creates. Production designers help inspire the sets, props, and costumes for a film. Storyboard and animatics designers help the director visualize each camera placement.

Most of the professionals who assist the director have their own staffs, all of whom come on board to make the director's vision succeed. Everyone on the set answers to the director. The director also selects post-production professionals such as composers, colorists, editors, engineers, and even film lab technicians.

The technology used in filmmaking has always advanced steadily, and yet at its core it is still a very old-fashioned industry. Cameras are, fundamentally, slightly updated copies of Thomas Edison's first prototypes.[86]

---

86. Edison's laboratories built a metal box with bits of glass on the front. Light shone into the box and onto strips of celluloid or plastic film. Chemicals on the film were affected by the light, and when dunked in other

LIVE-ACTION 35MM

Most cinema projectors take a 35mm reel, so nearly all films are shot on 35mm film stock, which is then edited into the 35mm master that is used to create all the prints sent to theaters. The actual width of the frame requires large lenses that can put a perfectly controlled image at pin-sharpness directly on the moving film, and they must be very accurately ground so that no imperfections appear in the high level of detail that the film can capture.

Many early films, most notably the larger epic pictures, were filmed on 70mm stock, but modern advances in the technology have enabled 35mm to deliver nearly the same clarity and saturation in a smaller frame. Some complex special effects sequences on expensive films are still filmed with 70mm cameras, but this is just to give extra resolution to the effects team, and the final print will end up on 35mm. Apart from IMAX films and on certain "ride films," 70mm is rarely used.

---

chemicals, these changes become fixed. The film was then threaded into another box with glass on the front, and when light was shone through it, a moving picture appeared on the wall as the celluloid strips were cranked through the box. Advances in engineering have made cameras that are more precisely manufactured and can accommodate larger magazines. Lenses are now sharper and cleaner. New chemical processes have resulted in film stocks that are clearer and brighter, and now can capture colors, as well. Electric motors have been invented, which enable cameras to run at a constant speed, silently, so that sound can be recorded on set. However, there are no real fundamental changes.

16MM

16mm is roughly half the size of 35mm and contains roughly half the visual resolution. However, the cameras and lenses are smaller and lighter, and the film stock is cheaper. Most television dramas are filmed on 16mm or Super16 film. Super16 is physically the same width celluloid, but the emulsion is slightly wider on the inside and is generally of a finer grain. Some low budget films are shot on Super16 and then blown up to 35mm prints for distribution. Unfortunately, the very process of optically expanding the image and printing it to another size of film results in a downgrade in image quality.

Technically speaking, if a Super16 negative were digitized at a high enough resolution to take full advantage of its greater clarity and then digitally resized and printed directly to 35mm film, you would get far better results. But at the moment, the cost of digitally scanning, resizing, and outputting an entire feature would be probably be cost-prohibitive to anyone who couldn't afford to shoot on 35mm in the first place. At the moment.

VIDEO

Until recently, video cameras were used to shoot news, soap operas, cheap sitcoms, and cheap commercials, but as HDTV equipment has been tested and perfected over the years, it has been used for more high-profile projects. George Lucas spent tens of millions developing a digital camera to film *Attack of the Clones*, and the results looked like a video-game cut-scene—not very impressive. Other films have experimented with digital and have had less than stellar results. Some exceptions exist. While digital cameras have proven that they can perform as well as film, they have yet to surpass traditional film technology for feature filmmaking. See Appendix B for more information on HD.

However, this will change. While anything remotely approaching the color depth and resolution of film requires proprietary camera technology with dedicated technicians re-working data and gear as the situations requires, Cheaper HD cameras and recording media are getting better. However, it will be some time before the best technology that can truly rival film for image quality is widely used, or even available, let alone affordable. That is why film cameras are still the choice of the discriminating pros.

Nevertheless, lately there has been a lot of hype regarding new consumer hi-def cameras for the guerrilla filmmaker, and a number of advertisements with famous directors endorsing home editing packages. There seems to be a feeling that now virtually *anyone* could make a major blockbuster in his backyard on a single laptop, but the reality is not so simple. You cannot shoot with digital consumer cameras and get the same results as 35mm film.

Now, you certainly could edit a feature film on Adobe Premiere or Final Cut Pro, but few professionals ever entertain the idea. It's technically feasible, but you wouldn't do it for the same reasons that nobody races the Grand Prix in a nice Dodge Caravan, no matter how current. You could complete the race, but the big boys have expensive post-production gear for reasons that go beyond snobbery.

This isn't to say that the digital revolution isn't shaking up the film industry. Everyone in Hollywood knows that pro-sumer technology is what the filmmakers of tomorrow will learn their craft on, and even as they do so the gap between professional film and consumer video is shrinking, particularly in the areas of effects and animation.

ANIMATION

Prosumer technology is what the filmmakers of tomorrow will learn their craft, particularly in the areas of effects and animation.

Animation has been changed drastically by the advances of modern computing. In the old days, Disney-style 2D animation was drawn on paper with a pencil one frame at a time, traced onto transparent celluloid where it was then painted, and the individual cels were laid onto a background and photographed, again, one frame at a time. It was an intensely difficult process with a number of complex, time-consuming steps, requiring whole armies of "tweeners," tracers, and painters to support the animators.

With most modern computer-based cel animation systems, the animators draw single frames on paper, which are then scanned into a computer, where the characters are then colored-in with a click of the mouse, and then composited over backgrounds within the same program. While the animation itself is still a tedious business, the process of getting it from paper to screen is much simpler, faster, and more flexible.

Another old style that has been updated slightly is stop-motion, or clay animation. The best examples of this are Aardman's *Chicken Run* and the "Wallace and Gromit" series. Other films used stop-motion animation for more realistic effects, but these duties are largely being taken over by 3D computer animation.

Today, claymation can benefit from computer technology in a number of ways. Using a high-resolution digital still camera, a computer can capture and store the frames of an animation, allowing the animator to play back his work on set or even add and subtract frames to adjust his timing as he works. Posing characters over a bluescreen, separated from their miniature backgrounds, allows for a smaller studio and simpler camera and lighting set-ups. The blue background can be later replaced by a filmed background of props.

The number one change in the animation industry has undoubtedly been the development of 3D computer animation. Equally suited to photo-realistic special effects work (such as in *Jurassic Park*) or stylized children's films (*Toy Story*), 3D animation is one of the greatest developments for films since the invention of color. And I'm not just saying that as an animator.

In 3D animation, a prop or character is modeled in three dimensions using pretty standard, high-school-level geometry. Objects can be built out of triangles, cubes, spheres, whatever geometric shapes suit the final product. The objects are then covered with any texture or material the animator designs, and placed in front of a virtual camera and lights. Characters are rigged with an internal skeleton of animation controls that allow them to be manipulated like a puppet. The character can be animated over a number of key frames, and the computer handles the in-between frames automatically. Animators preview their sequences by telling the computer to make a rough clip of the sequence, which computers can do quickly.

If the preview animation looks good, the sequence of frames is rendered in high resolution. This means the computer is asked to make a final calculation of each sequence, including every high-resolution detail. Depending on how complex the rendering engine is, it can take almost every physical effect of light and matter into consideration. Soft shadows, reflections, refractions, fog, atmospheric scatter, bounced light, translucency, caustics, light attenuation, lens distortion... everything required to simulate realism in the final image. Each frame is rendered separately, complex shots taking hours or days to render per frame.

The most interesting thing about computer animation is the availability and the affordability of some of the software programs. For example, ten years ago, computer animation was owned solely by large effects houses like Industrial Light

& Magic. The mere eleven minutes of 3D dinosaur footage for *Jurassic Park* (1993) were created with millions of dollars in computing power, driven by proprietary programs coded by ILM technicians over years of research and development.

One evidence of the possibilities afforded to independent filmmakers through the creative use of inexpensive software is the 2002 feature-length *Jimmy Neutron*. This studio release received an Academy Award nomination for Best Animated film. It was created entirely using off-the-shelf software (Lightwave 3D), readily available from any video production reseller for under $1,000. It should be pointed out that the studio purchased numerous licenses of the same software for numerous animators, and then numerous computers to assist in the rendering of the final frames. The budget for the film was $25 million, a fraction of which was animation gear. It earned a reported $80 million at the box office.

But even the high-dollar software programs developed (in part) by ILM are now for sale, and these days they can run on virtually any recent PC. With fast processors and powerful 3D accelerators becoming cheaply available to the consumer market, it can be a simple matter to set up an animation studio now.

And even 2D animation is easier to get into. A number of TV shows and commercials have been produced using Adobe's Flash program, which was originally developed (and is still widely used) to create and display simple text and graphic animation on Web sites. Today's desktop computers have the power and storage to serve most needs in the post-production process.

One of the biggest needs being served by animation software is in creating photo-realistic elements for post-production. These elements may be planes, submarines, or other expensive props. The elements may include weather phenomena like storms, choppy seas, or tornadoes. If the animators are clever enough, the elements include photo-real synthetic actors who can serve as stunt men or as soldiers in large computer-generated armies.

POST-PRODUCTION

Digital "post," as post-production is known for short, is bringing about a new stage of filmmaking, and the budding filmmaker needs to know about its capabilities. Post companies usually have digital tape machines and film playback machines for taking anything that was created in the field (the "production" stage), and transferring it into fast computers manned by highly artistic technicians. It is in these computers that the footage is improved, fixed, or altered in other creative ways. Post is expensive. But well-planned post-production images may save a filmmaker millions of dollars. George Lucas experimented creatively with post in the 1980s when he used the first computer compositing programs to replace skies, backgrounds, and unwelcome skylines in the television series *The Young Indiana Jones.* Lucas also experimented with computer-generated sets and props.

On the film *The Patriot,* it was cheaper for director Roland Emmerich to digitally insert hundreds of 3D British soldiers into empty landscapes than to hire and outfit a few more extras. The soldiers were computer images created by computer animation programs. Few filmgoers ever suspected that the humble extra had been replaced for such straightforward scenes in so simple a film. Emmerich also inserted period skylines and period buildings for historic Charlestown South Carolina, saving millions on set construction.

Admittedly, the technology used by Emmerich was hardly new, and the techniques were also time-tested and widespread. The interesting thing is that this was the first time that it was cheaper to create digital armies in post than to hire an extra division of Revolutionary re-enactors.

Cheaper technology will undoubtedly first be used to create cheaper B-movies filled with better monsters and flashier spaceships and other expensive-looking effects. But the wise director will use it to enhance his A-film and save money in the process.

Peter Jackson's *Lord of the Rings* used "invisible effects" to enhance the visuals. *Lord of the Rings* was such an effects-heavy series of films that it would be easy to overlook some of the digital enhancements less obvious than balrogs and massive armies.

Almost every shot in all three movies had some digital tweaking done to it. Cloudy skies were replaced with clear ones (or vice versa), slightly out-of-focus shots were sharpened, partial sets were extended, and daytime scenes were desaturated and darkened to look like night. More interestingly, almost every shot was also color-corrected. Any shot that could get more emphasis from being darkened, lightened, recolored, or sharpened was treated.

This is known as a digital intermediate, and it is becoming more and more common for studio films. It's only disadvantage is that every frame of the movie must be reprinted onto 35mm film. In Jackson's case, he had the facilities in-house to handle that. As a result, the film's director of photography was able to go into the computer and see how his shots were looking in sequence and with the effects. He was then able to adjust them further, so that any change that he might not have been able to achieve on-set could be controlled.

Does this mean the Director of Photography was incompetent on the set and used the computers to correct his errors? No, Andrew Lesnie is a master of his art. The corrections were enhancements to compliment the artistic messages in the script or to add things to the final image that would have been impossible or too expensive to achieve on set.

Filmmakers working outside of Hollywood need to full take advantage of digital post-production technologies to compete with films that have larger budgets. Most independent films can't compete with massive Hollywood productions when it comes to principle photography. Your equipment will pale in comparison to the vast resources used on the average studio picture. Your technicians and artists may not have the experience of Hollywood professionals.

This is why your script and pre-production process must be better, but you can also use a streamlined and powerful digital post to add more quality to your film. Most studio projects are onlined using million-dollar software and hardware suites, but if you have the time you can get the same or better results with Adobe After Effects, which retails for about $1,000.

Furthermore, films shot on digital cameras can have a full digital intermediate for no extra cost, unlike the large scanning budget required for projects shot on 35mm. I suggest that you read *The DV Rebel's Guide* by Stu Maschwitz if you have any interest in the technical side of digital cinematography, effects, color grading, or mastering.

Chapter 10
THE EASY THINGS TO LEARN

*Everything, really, at the end of the day is about
material: script script script script script. And if
you have the script, making the movie; the physical
making of the movie, given the fact that you're with
a professional group, is relatively straightforward and
extremely enjoyable.   —Ridley Scott*

The actual mechanics of getting pictures on film that can be cut together in such a way that the human eye can follow the progress of characters in a story is fairly simple. There are very basic rules that can be followed which will result in a very acceptable, straightforward style.

SHOOTING TECHNIQUE

The ability to take a crew onto a set and tell the lighting team where to set up, the sound guys what to expect, the actors where to stand, and the camera when to roll is not hard. It takes time and practice to become good at it, but it's just as simple as assigning plays to a football team. The technique involved mainly has to do with how the camera is placed and which images are shot on set.

Hopefully, by this stage, most of your film has been storyboarded and planned to perfection. You should know precisely what needs to be in each shot and why. In the storyboarding process, which is vital, you work out each shot visually. A storyboard looks like a comic strip. If the strip *Calvin and Hobbes*, for example, was a storyboard, the crew would know exactly how to set up the gear for each shot and scene.

Calvin's bathtub scene is very straightforward. The Calvin-coming-home-from-school scene places the camera on the right-hand side of the door, very near the house. It's a telephoto lens shot, with cumulus clouds and high-flying birds in the background. When Calvin is being bored in school, he might sit facing left of screen. When he inevitably is sent to the principal's office, he walks to the right of screen.

If camera locations and the actions of the actors are not properly devised, the story will make no coherent sense once it is edited. Some directors who work with small crews and serve as their own editors and cameramen, most notably Robert Rodriguez, only put key scenes on paper and keep the rest in their heads.

This type of mental filmmaking takes great ability and practice and I can't really recommend it for beginning filmmakers, even though I believe that Rodriguez's final product is often a good example of excellent direction. A good director should storyboard everything so that the entire crew sees how every shot contributes to the theme and message of his story.

VISUAL STORYTELLING

The visual vocabulary that is used in stringing events together in a film is an interesting area of study. There's a lot of room for personal expression, but leaving the beaten track too far behind can confuse your audience. By the same token, sticking too close to the tried-and-true, overused, or obsolete norms of Hollywood cutting styles may give you a stale product with no life of its own.

Figuring out what works and what doesn't is based largely on practice and experience. Most of it can be done (and must be done) in the early storyboards, but a lot of it will come down to the final cut, with many decisions made in editing.

Should there be a long shot here, or a close-up? Both shots look fine, technically speaking, but does the audience need to see the character's eyes here? Would it be more effective to show the long shot of the character standing alone? The dialogue and context have set the scene, so the audience knows the story... but how can pictures help tell *more* of the story, or tell it in a stronger way?

Nora Ephron, specializing in modern tales of sentimentality, uses visually simple techniques.[87] Despite their simplicity, her films have a reputation for being free from glaring technical directorial errors. They are filled with midshots from stationary cameras. The storyboards are not dissimilar from a simple comic strip. Every time a character speaks, the camera cuts just a little closer to that person. During more emotional moments, it cuts a little closer again. There is no fancy avant-garde camera movement here.

Her films work well using that style, because they are about people. Her plots are simple and the actors drive them. The stories are personal, and audiences get attached to the characters. At no point does the camera work or the cutting style pull the audience away from the characters or distance them from the story. Her gentle directorial technique never reminds the audience that they are watching a film, and allows her worldview to very subtly influence popular culture.

One of the most successful anti-Christians in Hollywood is Quentin Tarantino. His films are rife with pagan themes which reflect the moral bankruptcy of the filmmaker himself. For his repellent *Kill Bill* films, he went to a lot of trouble to get obvious, memorable shots, often at great expense. He built sets with removable ceilings so that he could hang Steadicam operators from cranes and get gigantic, sweeping moves. He constructed special lighting

---

87. *Sleepless in Seattle* (1993), *You've Got Mail* (1998).

rigs and interspersed scenes with animation and black and white photography. He even cut away from action at specific times so the audience wasn't sure exactly what had happened. The director's nihilistic pop-culture philosophy is manifest even in his technique.

The editing both supported the story and distracted from it. Under the circumstances, this is not a bad thing. The audience for *Kill Bill* was mostly made up of tween-age male fans of Tarantino who consider themselves connoisseurs of stylistic film technique. Also, the film itself was a near-plotless spoof/homage of cheesy kung-fu serials, so the particular brand of incoherent action filmmaking was itself the main point, and its worldview very overtly and offensively influenced popular culture.

Every project requires a different approach. A good director will know what that is without having to experiment, and that comes largely from experience. While the topics in this chapter are easy to learn, that doesn't necessarily mean that they are quick to learn. However, it's simple to get yourself a camera and an editing program for your computer, and practice shooting and cutting to tell a story. It's easy to practice, so practice.

EQUIPMENT

Almost every piece of equipment is easy to learn to use. Compared to the tricky artistic things involved in making films, virtually every piece of gear, from the cameras to the post-production computers, is not hard to use. However, knowing them and mastering them are two different things.

Also, there may not be a need to know everything about everything. For most directors, a complete working knowledge of how many amps each light on the grid will need and how to rig them for the control he needs is not necessary. A good director will know which lights do what, though, so he can make more intelligent suggestions to the lighting team and cinematographer faster and in reference to actual equipment.

Equipment can be learned quickly if you pay attention and take notes. Ask about other makes of equipment that do the same job. Don't learn the idiosyncrasies of how a specific mixing board works; learn the basics of what the board actually does and why that is required. A grasp of the underlying functions that equipment in general must provide will allow you to better understand it and learn it faster. Also, it gives you a better start in learning the newer gear that will replace it.

From a purely technical standpoint, there are set right and wrong answers to any mechanical film question. It's hard to get lost in the mire of artistic ambiguity when dealing with the mere technical side of image and sound quality. There is a definite level of professionalism that must be reached for every aspect of the project for it to look like it was put together by competent technicians.

When creating video projects for television broadcast, most stations have very rigorous requirements for technical excellence. It's in their best interests to air something that won't lower the standards of their image, so they use scopes and diagnostic instruments to measure the quality of the video signal. They make sure the blacks are truly black, the whites are truly white, and that the colors are strong without bleeding into each other. The audio channels must all be at a proper, consistent level, and the stereo separation must be clean, in phase, and noise-free.

Regardless of how artistically pleasing the program itself might be, or how interesting its content is, there are technical levels of excellence that must be reached. When a television show is transmitted, the signal strength of the audio and video must not be too weak, or they will be further degraded and even the least critical audience member will notice a flickering, faltering, fuzzy, obviously unprofessional product.

If you are making a program for a specific broadcaster, give that broadcaster a sample of work made on the equipment you intend to use in production. Ask the engineers to check the sample tape or DVD for technical fidelity. If it's not up to scratch, find out where the problem and how to fix it.

This is even more important for features that have been shot digitally. Your HD camera is significantly inferior to film, so you must be very careful not to lose any image quality during your post production process. If you plan to print your digital cut to film for theatrical release you will have to conduct a very careful color correction process to make sure that you have retained the highest level of color depth possible.

Film projects are no different. Test your gear. Shoot and process samples of the film stock you will be buying. Make sure you have a good match between professionals and every piece of equipment that will be used on the shoot. Also check to see that there is professional compatibility between the professionals you hire. Build a good team that will be a pleasure to work with.

You must strain for the highest quality product. Audiences have high standards for something they have paid $12 or more to see. They can tell the difference between *Saving Private Ryan* and the made-for-television war movie that was on Channel 5 last night. Technical quality is very easily measured. If your sound is crisp, your lighting is good, your camera-work is fluid and not confusing, your editing never jolts your viewers into remembering that they are watching a movie—then you have a technically passable product.

If you can do that, you're on the correct side of the G/C scale (good vs. cheap). Anything that tips the scale to the cheap side is relegated to faded cardboard boxes in Blockbuster Video, or late-night reruns on local cable channels. The directors who produce such content will probably end up making game shows for television.

Once you're on the right side of that scale, everything you can add to further tip the scale in the right direction is art. Everything creative or different that builds on the correct side of competency is what will gradually improve your status from a good director to a great director.

Chapter 11
THE HARD THINGS TO LEARN

Growing up I had this idea that the way animated films were made was that one night Walt would just sit upright in bed and say, "Dumbo!" and from that point on it was just a matter of doing what was in his brain. This is not anywhere near the truth. These films really begin with an idea, and then they change and they grow and they evolve into something stronger and better. —Pete Docter

Assuming that any reasonably bright and focused person can quickly learn the technical side of production, what are the other critically important lessons?

Most of these are related to those character lessons you will have learned at the family hearth and in struggling to make your first small projects. Others are related to your pursuit of nobility. Character is difficult to learn. It takes time, which is why the lessons are best begun at home, when one is under the supervision of honest parents who can say, "you're getting off track. Excellence lies in the other direction." Character is a foundation of wisdom, which will provide a director the unique ability to discern the extremes of good and evil, wisdom and folly.

A wise director will also be able to recognize art, which is a combination of an orderly reflection of an orderly worldview, the highest quality craftsmanship, and an edifying impact on the viewer.

A capable director will develop the ability to recognize the sublime, defined by Webster as "a grand or lofty style; a style that expresses lofty conceptions. The sublime rises from the nobleness of thoughts, the magnificence of words, or the harmonious and lively turn of the phrase; to raise on high; to exalt; to heighten; to improve."

Film has the ability to do this. For more than half a century, film content has been doing the opposite, driving civil society downward in a vulgar and common direction. Thus, the film industry is now weak and exhausted of vital energy. Directors can choose projects that elevate all that is noble and civil, and they can create on the screen those emotional moments that lift men's souls higher.

This, of course, is not possible unless the director has a vision for virtue. Seek virtue and study nobility.

A capable director will have an obvious ability to lead men and inspire men to greatness. The contributions of a talented staff will be all the greater if the director can get top performance from all of them. Effective leadership is a concept that is hard enough to describe, let alone teach or duplicate. Military and business leaders have yet to discover the full range of ingredients that make up a commanding leader. But they do agree that respect and obedience are granted to those who have character as well as capability, especially the character to be concerned for the welfare of those under his authority.

Finally, a good director will have the maturity and ability to improve his weaknesses through humility and collaboration. Even inexperienced directors can succeed if they can extract wisdom and knowledge from talented crews. If they can recruit the best and then recognize good contributions when they are properly given, the production benefits. Keeping a creative environment creative will be one of the more rewarding fruits of good directing.

WHAT HOLLYWOOD KNOWS THAT YOU DON'T

Experience is an asset that is almost impossible to over-value. When it comes to the day-to-day tasks of making a story appear on celluloid, good solid experience trumps flash-in-the-pan brilliance any day. The mechanics of technically superior filmmaking have been honed to a fine art in some Hollywood circles.

Professional excellence in acting is difficult to obtain without experience. Even the most vapid Hollywood starlet chosen for her million-dollar smile (and other physical attributes) will have at her elbow, directly off screen, a brilliant acting tutor and a skilled dialogue coach, both of whom are highly experienced. Producing a good performance as an actor or coaching a good performance as a director is a difficult thing to learn, and Hollywood knows how this is done.

Each actor, character, role, and project is different. Experience with different circumstances is what makes it possible for a director to get consistently good results, regardless of circumstances, on schedule and on budget.

The key to good acting on the screen is subtlety. This is a direct counterpoint to stage acting, where voices must be projected to the back of the theater and gestures should be visible to the most distant seat. Experienced film actors have mastered the art of quiet subtlety. Film directors must know exactly how to balance the intensity and subtlety of a good performance. Too much subtlety makes the performance fall flat. Too little results in overacting. It is very difficult for beginning directors to get this balance right.

Because today's production techniques have grown out of the large "studio" system, specialists still tend to specialize and Hollywood knows how to integrate these people into a well-oiled, professional machine. This machine can be intimidating to outsiders.

INTEGRATION OF THE DISCIPLINES

From an integration standpoint, one film where everything contributes and fits together properly is *Back to the Future*

(1985). Apart from one or two lines that feel slightly out of place, the entire movie fits together and plays perfectly. The acting is good, the casting is superb, the scenes are interesting and exciting, the editing keeps everything running right in tune with what the audience wants to see, and the special effects look great, even by today's standards.

The script is technically tight and solidly coherent, partly because Robert Zemeckis (the director) and Bob Gale (the writer) spent so much time on it. It was the one script that they could not get any interest in, and so while they made *I Wanna Hold Your Hand*, *Used Cars*, and wrote the story for *1941*, they continued to work on it. Finally, after the success of *Romancing the Stone*, they had the reputation and contacts they needed. During this time, they had grown as filmmakers, and the final *Back to the Future* script owed a lot to their recent experience.

The story was originally inspired by Bob Gale seeing his father's high-school yearbook, and was written by compiling scenes that they themselves wanted to see (modern rock played in the '50s, a skateboard chase, etc.). As time went on, these scenes were assembled into a script and streamlined until it was ready for production. It had a good premise and structure, memorable characters, strong plot moments, and a solid ending.

Steven Spielberg signed on as executive producer and helped hone the script even more. Early drafts had the time machine as a refrigerator, which then became a DeLorean.

Then the climax involved Marty driving into the desert to intercept a plutonium core from an atom bomb being tested. Finally, the far superior concept of tying everything to the courthouse clock tower was devised.

Eric Stoltz was originally cast in the role of Marty, but Robert Zemeckis realized the he, although a fine actor, wasn't working in the part or with his co-stars. Zemeckis looked at C. Thomas Howell and Canadian pop star Corey Hart, and then finally went to the producers of "Family Ties" and asked that they allow Michael J. Fox (his first choice) to take the role.

With Michael J. Fox working on set, his character developed new depth. His experience in television comedy helped him make Marty McFly more endearing and Christopher Lloyd was able to tweak his character to match. With these two solid leads working in harmony with each other and the framework of the script, the tone of the movie changed slightly and became lighter.

The '50s setting of the film was completed by talented costumers, builders, and set dressers, serving as a backdrop for comedy or action. The special effects of the film were limited, but effective and highly polished. The camerawork was slick and engaging. As the two Bobs filmed, they were able to weave all of these elements together into a truly great film.

Ian Silvestri then assembled the largest studio orchestra at the time to record the fanciful and adventurous score, which meshed with the final cut of the film. The editing of the film set the timing of the film at an exciting pitch, and the final product went on to be memorable, successful, and spawned two sequels.

Because the writer and director were technically experienced, they could have created a competent, professional-looking film even without some of these superior elements. However, their skill as storytellers and their artistic experience enabled them to make every aspect excellent. But this kind of integrated effort can also be seen on a smaller scale—when this same type of collaboration comes together to a make a powerful film moment more than a mere sum of its parts.

PINNING

Previously we discussed the power of unbelievers to take moral concepts, but to present them in a dangerously subversive way by mixing broad universal principles rooted in biblical Christianity with pagan applications. One example of this was the hugely successful film *Gladiator*, by director Ridley Scott, which mixed nobility, sacrifice, and love of family with a favorable presentation of false worship.

For the purpose of this discussion, however, *Gladiator* is a helpful tool to understand the concept of "pinning." Director Scott often talks about "pinning" a scene. What he's referring to is when multiple elements come together in a moment to make the scene stronger as a result. On the *Gladiator* DVD commentary, Scott talks about this in regard to the scene where Commodus murders Marcus Aurelius.

It's a tough scene, packed with foreboding and emotion. A lesser director might have just passed it off as a simple "evil son kills unsuspecting father," or even played it off-screen, but Scott wanted to use it as something which underscored the characters, something that would be a major film moment. This type of request is a nightmare for writer and actors.

The scene begins with Caesar bluntly informing his son that he will not be emperor. His son contains it well, but when he starts to ask why this honor will go to another, he breaks down and weeps. He brokenly asks his father what he has done wrong, why he isn't considered trustworthy, and Joaquin Phoenix delivers this beautifully-written speech exceptionally well.

The acting is superb, not just because Phoenix accurately portrays an emotional meltdown, but because his actions convey more information than his words. He's asking about his responsibilities as a leader, but what's on his mind and heart are his confused emotions regarding himself, Rome, his father, and his rival Maximus. Far more comes out in his performance than just the bitter disappointment on the script page.

The script says that Caesar is deeply moved, and tries to comfort his son, but Commodus is so emotionally amped by this point that he kills his father. But the scene wasn't really working. Richard Harris suggested that the scene needed "a pinning," and provided the line that completed it himself.

As the father sees his son's inner turmoil and frustration, he admits that he is to blame, and kneels before him, begging pardon. "Commodus," he confesses, "Your flaws as a son is my failure as a father." At that moment the son, seeing his father kneeling on the floor and taking responsibility for his own corruption, kills him.

That one line provided the audience with immense insight into both characters and served to further motivate Commodus's act of patricide. Actor Richard Harris's great experience in cinema enabled him to see what the scene was lacking, and his exceptional understanding of the character showed him what could complete it, which in this case was something that even the writer had not understood or planned.

At that pivotal moment in the movie, Richard Harris pinned the scene, giving it a set point that the rest of the film and its crew could hinge on. Not only did it give the audience a flash of revelation, it inspired Joaquin Phoenix with a better understanding of his character. It gave Hans Zimmer an emotionally strong moment that supported, and was supported by, the score that he wrote for that moment. A weaker scene would have made such expressive music seem comically over the top, but all the pieces of the puzzle came together and strengthened each other.

Essentially, it all comes back to experience. In order to be a great writer, director, or producer, you need to know what contributes to great film. You need to be able to understand from a script or a pitch or an uncut take what works, or what "plays." Understanding what does and what doesn't takes time to learn, but it can be learned. Much of it can be learned by watching good films in an analytical way. A lot of it can be learned by shooting simple stories on video and seeing how they can be cut together. There is no substitute for experience in communicating with audiences.

WHAT YOU KNOW THAT HOLLYWOOD DOESN'T

Hollywood's highly-experienced, collaborative machine is not invincible, and is particularly susceptible to well-planned guerrilla warfare.

Films can be made without using the big systems and the big crews. If you make a few small video projects, you'll get a feel for the flexibility of a one-man-band production. These are by no means ideal, but the enterprising writer/producer/ director can make a movie that finds wide distribution.

The story of Robert Rodriguez's experience with the stylized film *El Mariachi* is now legendary (as well as his production work on its increasingly violent and sensual sequels). Though strongly not recommended as an uplifting Christian film, there are many lessons which can be derived from studying the innovation surrounding the production of this film.

Rodriguez served as cameraman, director of photography, director, sound recordist, film loader, stunt coordinator, pyrotechnics engineer, writer, producer, casting director, editor, and sound mixer.

His crew also did double-duty as his actors, he shot it in his own town, and his budget was under ten thousand dollars. Because his crew/actors were mostly Mexican, the final film's dialogue is all in Spanish. Nevertheless, his final film was very well received by American rental patrons who liked the action, and also by the art-house "intellectuals" who were convinced that because it was a foreign-language film it must be packed with deep symbolism! Rodriguez laughs now that the supposedly most symbolic images in his film are there merely because they made for interesting cutaways to cover unsynchronized dialogue.

But for all the attention that Hollywood producers pay to foreign cinematic trends and music video directors and successful authors, Hollywood's ideas mostly come from Hollywood. Today's films are often retreads of the same plots and genres from recent history, or remakes of earlier films and television shows.

If you make small video productions and succeed, you'll easily learn what Rodriguez did; you'll know better than Hollywood what can be done with the faith, resourcefulness, and the friends and family that helped you with your first productions. More importantly, you will know that you can bring new, better ideas.

If you have allowed yourself to be trained by the intensity and struggle of moral tests, you'll know how to write these convincingly into the backstory of your moral heroes. Moral tests are formidable in real life to those who have tender consciences. Moral tests must be formidable in the fictional life of your hero. The more moral tests you pass as a young adult, the more empathetic understanding you will have for your hero.

You will also know from living attentively in a close-knit family what the extremes of character can be. These, too, will increase the depth of character in your heroes, and the lack of good character in your villains.

If you have dug deeply into history, you'll know about the providential course of history and how a sovereign Creator works to plan the lives of real people. The real people in your scripts will be much more real than Hollywood's caricatures of humanity.

If you are a Christian, you will understand the truths of human nature better, especially the deceitfulness and darkness of sin. Your understanding of the costs of redemption will help you write authentic redemption into your stories, which is one of the most sought-after truths by audiences worldwide.

Audiences want to see your hero wake up and grow up. Near the end of the film, he does. This is called his self-revelation moment. He "gets it." Or he repents of his great hindering weakness or folly. He changes his mind. As we discussed in chapter seven, he realizes the theme of the film. Your version of truth comes out in this moment. This is why people go to see movies. They want to grow up too. They want to be taught the truth. They are looking for it in the films they see and they want to get to a point of maturity with their heroes.

Your stories can teach the truth in every scene. You can show the negative consequences of bad behavior. You can show the proper roles of protagonist—the good guy—and the antagonist—the bad guy. Many films get it backward today, usually on purpose. You can have a purpose, too, for every scene and every character. Every virtue can be supported rather than vilified. See how gratifying it is to your audience to root for the good guys and boo the bad guys, for a change. When they clash, let the collision between good and evil be resounding. The losers need to lose instead of being lionized.

The audience will enjoy it, and so will you. But no matter how much fun you have in creating stories that teach the truth, remember that films are not primarily an entertainment medium. They are weapons. If you understand that, then you are ready to pursue filmmaking as a vocation.

Chapter 12

THE FUTURE OF FILMMAKING OUTSIDE HOLLYWOOD

*One day, some little fat girl in Ohio is going to
be the new Mozart and make a beautiful film
with her father's camcorder and the so-called
professionalism about movies will be destroyed forever.
—Francis Ford Coppola* [88]

Leaders like you cannot chart the future of filmmaking
unless you know the weaknesses and errors of the past.
The industry surrendered to the dogmas of the Frankfurt
School. The industry allowed Gramsci to march through
the cinematic institutions.[89] As his colleagues discipled

---

88. Quoted by Rob Kenner, "Are effects really that special?" (The Observer: February 2000).

89. Gramsci was the revolutionary who articulated the "long march through the institutions," meaning a takeover of all centers of influence so that the minds of all Westerners could be prepared psychologically for socialist revolution.

the industry, traditional culture disintegrated worldwide. This small but powerful industry has been led, controlled, and influenced by a relatively small group of men who operate from a small geographic area. As we have learned, the so-called "Hollywood system" is fraternal, arrogant, intellectually cowardly, and politically deceived.

The system is neither ashamed of, nor secretive about, its own narcissistic society. For more than fifty years, it has perpetuated a reputation for ruthlessly hoarding the power it wields, and for lavishly spreading a sophisticated debauchery in order to preserve and affirm its stubborn ideology. This is why you are never likely to break into it successfully. Fortunately, you won't have to in order to make influential films.

Three recent developments challenge the cultural and financial hegemony of the Hollywood system: the Internet, inexpensive production technology, and a new generation of literate filmmakers. Hollywood is not dying, but it is being overshadowed by exploding numbers of competing productions and a cultural change in the way films are distributed. Just look at a few basic numbers and trends. How many films did Hollywood make last year? Fewer than three hundred. Almost half that number were made in British Columbia, a two-hour plane flight north of Hollywood. Elsewhere in the U.S., more than one thousand were made. Elsewhere in the world, more than five thousand were made. At the moment, Hollywood still sets the cultural tone because people expect it to. But filmgoers will be getting smarter. And at that point, Hollywood slips into oblivion.

REVERSE COLONIZATION

Hollywood has "colonized" the worldview of the world for two generations. People from Tokyo to Oslo have been taught how to think and feel and be politically correct. As other production centers begin to distribute electronically, Hollywood will begin to lose its shadowy hold on the minds of moviegoers. In Lagos, Nigeria, for example, Hollywood blockbusters gather dust on the shelves of video stores as customers rent African features on DVD and videocassette. Nigerian filmmakers are creating their own stories now, with video gear and original scripts. Production quality is not to a high standard, but neither are the budgets. Comparisons matter little, since Hollywood has lost popularity.

In 2004, more than 2,500 local features were made in this up-and-coming production town, which now employs some 200,000 film crew workers. There are no unions and no government subsidies. It is a free-market phenomenon with free agents who know exactly what their public wants to see. Their films are popular with Africans. Their films are making money. Hollywood is about to be swamped with competition like this in other nations. Soon, Hollywood will no longer influence films being made in these centers because they will have created their own grammar of film and their own worldview. The big question of the twenty-first century is one of cultural colonization. Who will be discipling moviegoers with new stories?

Perhaps you can now see why this book has been so blunt and straightforward about the teaching power of film and the responsibilities that go with teaching. You could spend a career at the bottom of the ladder in a culturally irrelevant movie town named Hollywood, or you could be showing tomorrow's filmmakers how to tell good stories that break Hollywood's iron cage of cultural conformity. You could play a role in the reverse colonization of the world.

Film producers in Bombay, India, are now making one thousand films per year, with average films returning twenty times their production costs. They realize the coming worldwide influence their films will have. Indian actresses believe they will soon be setting the worldwide standards for the definition of feminine beauty. This is likely; not just because they are beautiful, but because that beauty will grace more silver screens than any other variety of beauty. Political analysts understand the influence of Indian film on the Muslim world, where it is far more popular than Western film, and speculate on the direction that influence will take. So do many up-and-coming Islamic filmmakers. Just how influential will Bollywood's media influence be?

INFOTAINMENT

The future of film's vast influence will no longer be limited to theaters and television. According to Nicholas Negroponte, director of the Massachusetts Institute of Technology Media Lab, people with Internet connections will become mini television studios and film distributors without middlemen. People with fiber-optic access to the Internet will be able to buy and download precisely the kind of entertainment they want. The people who control these trends will possess skills in computer-related media arts. Indian businessmen point out that there are now more information technologists in India than in any other nation.

As India combines this knowledge base with the development of film, they will be a gargantuan world influence. They are currently surveying the ways they can take advantage of the vast Chinese market, which already has an appetite for Indian film. Chinese filmmakers intend to follow similar patters of mass distribution of infotainment. The demands of the combined market will certainly set cultural trends for more than a century. By 2050, the demands of this audience will so far outstrip the appetites of American consumers that Hollywood hegemony will be a quaint historical curiosity. So will television and telephones, as they are replaced by broadband alternatives. Yes, the population of America will have increased to some four hundred million by then, but China and India will stand at three *billion*, and they expect to be connected and ready for the interactive virtues of the infotainment world. What will they want?

DOMONETICS

Whatever it is they want, they will be able to get, down to very niche-oriented specifics. In 1969, Alan Kiron, a staff scientist at the U.S. Patent Office, coined the term "domonetics" to describe the interactions between culture and technology.[90] Chinese Web surfers will learn how to get around the barriers set up by a nervous government and they will hit the sites that give them what they want, making *electronic connections from their domiciles*. Domonetics is the perfect word to describe the way they will introduce themselves to freedom, new ideas, and personal technological power.

George Gilder described this world-changing opportunity. "The force of microelectronics will blow apart all the monopolies, hierarchies, pyramids, and power grids of established industrial society," he wrote a decade ago, and events are proving his thesis. "It will undermine all totalitarian regimes. Police states cannot endure under the advance of the computer because it increases the powers of the people far faster than the powers of surveillance.

"The new law of networks exalts the smallest coherent system: the individual human mind and spirit. A healthy culture reflects not the psychology of crowds but the creativity and inspiration of millions of individuals reaching for high goals. In place of the broadcast pyramid, a peer network will emerge in which all the terminals will be smart—not mere television sets but interactive video

---

90. George Gilder, *Life After Television* (New York, Norton, 1994), p. 57. The term combines the words "domicile." "connections," and "electronics." Kiron used the term to describe how work and living patterns would be reshaped by the new computer and other communications tools.

receivers, processors, and transmitters."[91]

Both the intelligent and the less so will always be entertained, challenged, taught, and informed by stories. Stories are for everyone. But the new technologies give smart people the freedom to get away from Hollywood indoctrination and seek out stories that are not "politically correct." Niche-market movies can tell the truth, and people are fascinated by truth. Especially people who have been denied it by Hollywood or by bamboo-curtain tyrants.

The flip side of this coin is that these new technologies also give consumers the freedom to find niche programming that is more politically correct, more false, and even more defiling that the Hollywood norm. Some of the largest internet industries have been pornographic, which has usually been the case with the new technologies such as home video recorders or the printing press. All technologies are tools that can be used in many ways.

Computer users in China are already using networked computers as windows into the free world. They are also turning their home computers into theaters, museums, classrooms, television studios, banking systems, shopping centers, post offices, and telephones that largely escape the censorship and control of the Chinese government. This computer-driven media revolution that is chipping away at this communist state could bury the very ugliest part of Hollywood—the mass psychology—and it will unearth

---

91. Ibid., p. 61.

what Hollywood buried—the civilized interests of individual people.

George Gilder described Hollywood's television legacy saying, it is "not vulgar because people are vulgar, it is vulgar because people are similar in their prurient interests and sharply differentiated in their civilized concerns. All of world industry is moving increasingly toward more segmented markets. But in a broadcast medium, such a move would be a commercial disaster. In a broadcast medium, artists and writers cannot appeal to the highest aspirations and sensibilities of individuals. Instead, manipulative masters rule over huge masses of people. Television is a tool of tyrants. Its overthrow will be a major force for freedom and individuality, culture and morality. That overthrow is at hand."[92]

Unfortunately, the cultural goals of most Western "indie" film producers are heavy on rebellious individuality and somewhat lacking in morality. Throughout liberal America, thousands of neo-marxists have grasped the promises of new technology and hope to use it to further communize the film industry. Most of them see an unfettered film community—freed from Hollywood's capitalistic limitations and "Puritanical" restrictions—as the perfect tool for individuals to express their own desires and messages outside of traditional conventions. This is apparent at most independent film festivals, where top-listed entries are

---

92. Ibid., pp. 48-49.

generally X-rated barrages of disconnected images and ideas, or glorifications of dysfunctional fatalism.

Both the form and function of some of these films exist merely to challenge and destroy traditional ideas of order. This is a very common trend among the "free-thinkers" of this new era of personal film. More accurately, it is a common trend among all "progressives" who have historically steered away from traditional and biblical order in search of their own goals. The individual freedom sought by post-modern philosophers, secular humanists, and most independent filmmakers would be more accurately regarded as anarchy for the sake of personal gratification.

This book has been very critical of the trends and ideas espoused by Hollywood and has called for the founding of an independent film industry. I admit that, on the surface, this message is very similar to the battle cries of the indie film movement; the loudest proponents of indie film are usually the loudest detractors of Hollywood. However, please do not misunderstand my position; most of the faults of Hollywood are just as prevalent in the Sundance crowd as they are among the big-studio moguls. Most of Hollywood's enemies are merely jealous or feel left out, and many others are simply opposed to the idea of capitalism and big business.

I strongly urge readers to examine very closely all the different factions of this new age of media, and their underlying ideologies, before blindly jumping onto the closest bandwagon and echoing the rhetoric of the wrong side. Fortunately, most of the readers of this book are in a unique position to understand the issues surrounding the changes which are occurring in the film industry.

THE PERCEPTIVE GENERATION

Frank Capra once commented, "In Hollywood we learn about life only from each others' pictures."[93] What would happen if a segment of the American population were to be raised outside of the dominant constrictive culture, were given freedom of thought and such a wide variety of disparate experiences that their imaginations were super-charged with the precise opposite of commonality, monotony, and tedium?

In the 1970s and '80s, a significant percentage of parents concluded that the state school apparatus would be as stifling to their children as it was for them. They dared to turn their backs on both the system and the culture of a normalized, collectivized upbringing. By teaching their children at home, many of their freed pupils learned to learn. They learned to be individuals. They learned to like learning and consequently discovered literature and experiences that have been closed to normalized Americans for decades.

Most of these young men and women read thousands of books before they learn to drive, and when they launch

---

93. Quoted by Hortense Powdermaker, Hollywood the Dream Factory: *An Anthropologist looks at the Movie Makers* (Boston: Little, Brown, 1950), p. 20.

out on their own adventures, they have little interest in heading for the perpetually adolescent culture perpetuated by American films.

Consequently, many of these young adults realize early that they will be creating cultures of their own design and making. Their marriages are different, their lifestyles reflect the freedom they have come to appreciate, and when their creativity is unleashed on their respective interests, the results are innovative, inventive, and originally artful.

This perceptive new generation is looking at the world from a fresh perspective. They have observations to make and stories to tell. Art is nothing more than an orderly way of looking at the world. These new artists/observers have the clear-eyed viewpoint necessary to show the world what it has failed to see for a very long time. Those of us who view their work will be liberated by what we see. We will want to see more.

This book has focused primarily on this new breed of moviemaker. If you did not have the unique opportunity of a home education, you can still continue to train your senses to discern the differences between the corrupt legacy of Hollywood and the promise of traditional storytelling. You will be part of this Perceptive Generation, which could become tomorrow's strongest creative force in filmmaking and the *strongest force in shaping the economic and political landscape of the future.*

Not only in communist nations, but in the socialist "democracies" of the West, the corrupt welfare state could be replaced as a result of this new information technological revolution, which will be driven by the content providers. The CEOs of every technology company from Silicon Graphics to Sony to Philips know that "content is king." Content is more important than any new hardware breakthrough. This is why it is important for you to attain your goal to be a literate writer/producer/director. Those who produce niche-market infotainment for the smart people at the receiving end of the information highway will create the culture and society of the next two hundred years. Authors James Dale Davidson and Lord Rees-Mogg describe this coming shift in their book *The Sovereign Individual.* "Now that information technology is displacing mass production it is logical to expect the twilight of mass democracy," by which they mean the managed economy envisioned by Karl Marx. "The crucial megapolitical imperative that made mass democracy triumph during the Industrial Age has disappeared. It is therefore only a matter of time until mass democracy goes the way of its fraternal twin, Communism."[94]

Readers of this book must be careful that they keep their goals in mind and not be sidetracked by sheer technological capability. As older forms of media and their underlying infrastructures are replaced by new media, we

---

94. James Dale Davidson and William Rees-Mogg, *The Sovereign Individual* (New York: Simon and Schuster, 1997), p. 311.

must ensure that our standards and methodologies, like our films, remain true to the highest standards of cultural and creative excellence.

SCALING THE PINNACLE OF CREATIVITY

The motion picture arts and sciences are a distillation of the highest artistic standards from a tight combination of the most creative professional disciplines. Every historical creative art and science is represented: music, fashion, acting, architecture, theology, composition, design, photography, and many others, including those which have been invented for film, such as cinematic lighting, editing, and directing.

One movie, in other words, demands a professional integration of the best art and the best technology and the best ideas.

The better modern films do combine the best of everything, except ideas. The ideas are mediocre and the ideology is almost universally corrupt or dishonest. This is where the perceptive generation comes in. Unafraid to state the obvious, unafraid to be moral, unafraid to be politically incorrect, their media will have the potential of the traditional heroism that filmgoers want to see.

Independent films can and will challenge the dreary politically-correct hegemony of the industry. If this new breed of filmmakers can succeed responsibly and artistically, Hollywood will be forced to share its power. It will be interesting to see if the coexistence is peaceful.

I have a prediction based on the recent skirmish between Mel Gibson and Hollywood which played out before and after the release of his controversial film *The Passion of the Christ*. At first, studio heads were furious and vowed to blacklist Gibson. After the film pulled in $120 million, however, some Hollywood execs spoke up for Gibson's freedom of artistic expression.[95]

Money talks in Hollywood, but the culture war is so intense, there can be no peaceful coexistence between worldviews. The reason this war is intense is well defined by economist Gary North in his 2004 book *The War Against Mel Gibson*:

> What do I mean by 'culture war'? I mean a battle for the visible marks of supremacy in all of those areas of life that reflect the first principle of a society...
>
> Culture is an extension of the cooperation of these three institutions. It encompasses the arts: music, painting, sculpture, and the graphic arts, including film. It encompasses the written word: literature and some forms of journalism. It encompasses food and all of the etiquette and ceremonies that accompany food. Culture reflects and reinforces men's opinions on five crucial issues: God, man, law, causation, and time. Culture surrounds modern man with a patchwork of competing visions and competing answers. The culture war exists

---

95. See articles by Sharon Waxman, *The New York Times*, February 26, 2004 and March 14, 2004. Since those first weeks, the film has gone on to earn an estimated one billion dollars worldwide.

because men do not agree on the answers to these questions. Who is God? What does He want mankind to do? What is man? To whom or what is mankind responsible? What are the rules governing men's life and death? What is the nature of historical cause and effect? Where are we headed? Where have we been?

Because there can be no peaceful coexistence between a film industry, be it Hollywood-centered or indie-driven, that answers these questions one way—and perceptive, honest filmmakers who answer these questions another, truthful way—a new film industry will emerge, driven by the perceptive generation.

OTHER TRENDS TO WATCH

In addition to Domonetics and Reverse Colonization, the biggest trend is intellectual freedom. The Internet has opened a window on truth for many in bamboo and iron curtain countries.

Worldwide home education has opened a similar window for young students who have escaped the oppressive pedagogy of forced, politically-correct schooling. This freedom has opened creative lines of thinking that would otherwise not have been freed. Most home-educated children plan to do the same for their children, allowing the home environment to become a place of exploration and intellectual discovery that will chart the course for greater creative expansion and expression in media.

Internet video sites like Youtube or GoogleVideo allow amateur filmmakers to share their own short films and compare notes with other users of the site. Independent Christian filmmakers may be able to take advantage of these technologies and use them for the glory of God. As broadband Internet connections become more widespread, there will be more video content on the Web, and it will be higher quality video. Recently we've seen DVD collections of canceled television series (such as *Family Guy*) selling well enough to push the show back into production, or in the case of *Firefly*, to fund a big-budget theatrical film. Eventually, for "edgier" content, the broadcast phase might be skipped, using Internet and cable for initial showings, and then DVD sales for revenue.

There also appears to be a small but growing market for shorts specifically for the Internet, although so far it's hard to tell exactly how to make any real money without a large corporate sponsor. The most popular Internet shorts so far were probably those in BMW's *The Hire* series. Each film was 5-7 minutes long, had a large budget, a full crew, and attracted a famous director, such as Guy Ritchie, John Frankenhiemer, Ang Lee, John Woo, or Tony Scott. Each film was downloadable in hi-res and with full DVD features, including director's commentaries. However, most internet shorts are merely webcammed exhibitions of stupidity.

With the growing sophistication of home theater systems and the spread of HDTV, there will be fewer reasons to go to the local multiplex at all. Eventually, direct-to-video titles may rent as well as their theatrically-released counterparts, if distribution companies recognize their potential. There will also always be a debate on how much effect Internet piracy has on box-office profits, but I don't think I'll address that or the copyright debate now, except to say this: As you "produce yourself," building the character and backbone that will make you a successful leader in the industry, don't compromise character at any point in your development. Don't steal intellectual property.

At the moment, the industry is fanatically attacking all forms of Internet file sharing that could possibly be used to pirate films, and is publishing staggering statistics of potentially lost revenue. Older readers will remember similarly pessimistic projections during the early 1980s, when videocassette recorders hit the home market. Now, of course, video rentals are a major source of income to distributors and producers alike, turning what would be dead inventory into a valuable commodity. Apple computer managed to turn Internet music into a profitable business, and has now expanded into tv shows and movies. Currently Amazon, Walmart, Netflix and others are selling and renting films over the Internet, but time will tell exactly how this pans out.

At the moment, what is possibly more effective to changing the balance of power in Hollywood is the proliferation of Web sites with information about films. Most of them are mainly celebrity gossip and fan-site interviews, but there is a growing list of sites that actually provide some very useful filmmaking resources. Mark Curtis and Scott Kirstner both have blogs documenting new developments and trends in technology and the industry.

The spoiler sites that publish information from "unnamed sources" about upcoming films, such as Harry Knowles's crudely-managed "Ain't It Cool News," are already having huge effect on the word-of-mouth that makes or breaks film releases. Studios stopped test screenings long ago, after the advent of e-mail and Web sites made it all too easy for randomly selected test audiences to instantly and globally spill the beans on a film's plot.

On the *Back to the Future* DVD, Robert Zemeckis explains how useful test screenings can be to judge audience response, and laments the fact that in today's world of camera phones and file sharing, it's just too risky to let an audience see a film before its release. But the Internet can also be a very powerful and positive marketing tool, as shown by Peter Jackson's *Lord of the Rings*.

Worried that die-hard Tolkien fans, upset at the liberties that Jackson was reportedly taking with the literature, would create a wave of negative Internet publicity, the PR staff released behind-the-scenes photos and granted exclusive interviews to several Tolkien-based Web sites. By the time *Fellowship of the Ring* was released, the Web fans had been completely won over by the attention they were receiving, and they contributed a great deal to the groundswell of positive word-of-mouth that helped make the film a success.

CHEAP AND CHEAPER TECHNOLOGY

With the advent of digital video technologies, you can now buy a consumer handicam that shoots HD for a few dollars a tape. Home PCs are now powerful enough and large hard drives cheap enough that editing large amounts of broadcast-quality footage is within most everyone's capability. However, there's a lot of hype about digital filmmaking being within everyone's grasp that should not be taken too seriously.

Creating a 35mm print of film-resolution images suitable for theatrical release is an arduous task which requires expensive equipment and skilled artisans. There are few shortcuts or easy avenues here. With the slow increases in HD movie channels on cable, made-for-TV movies shot on HD could become more prevalent, but the impact of these channels remains to be seen.

Digital cameras *are* becoming more common in the feature film industry, but those that are capable of filming rich images and recording uncompressed, hi-res footage are no cheaper than 35mm cameras to rent or buy, and for the moment require specialized technicians to operate. Their only current advantage is that the director can shoot more hours less expensively, there is no film development cost, and if extensive visual effects are required, the footage is already digitized.

Within five or ten years, filming a feature cheaply using non-proprietary digital cameras without a specialized crew will be commonplace, but the great cinematographers will still use film. Digital photography will be used for effects-heavy films, low-budget romantic comedies, and dramas where a rich filmic image is not required, and by rogue directors whose unorthodox shooting styles are best accommodated by digital gear.

Nevertheless, the cheaper video technology of today will greatly affect Hollywood. While consumer video cameras will not create the films of the future, they will be used to train the filmmakers of tomorrow. For a very low price, you can get a decent camera and editing suite, which is all that is required to start building and honing the techniques of visual storytelling. Check Appendix B for a short discussion of equipment issues.

FILMMAKING LITERACY

An inexpensive new educational tool is available for aspiring filmmakers. It's cheaper than film school and many filmmakers say that it's better. It's the the annotated and commentated DVD. With "making-of" footage, mini-featurettes, and director's commentaries now standard on most films released on DVD, there is a huge amount of material on the entire production process of almost every movie. A good director's commentary will not only explain how they did what they did, but why. They refer to earlier versions of the scripts, and why they changed what they did, and how that makes the film stronger. They describe how certain actors worked on certain parts, what they contributed, and how they were motivated.

For example, in the *Gladiator* commentary, Ridley Scott explains the foreshadowing of a heroic figure, what's on the deleted scenes and why they were deleted, the importance of script, and why a sexual relationship between Russell Crowe and Connie Neilson's characters would have been "immoral" and was deliberately avoided. Scott's is a great commentary because you get insight into the making of the film and you hear Scott's handpicked colleagues describe why they made specific professional and artistic choices.

This proliferation of good information is making the study and understanding of film more popular, but usually on a superficial and snobbish level. There is also a growing popularity of film art books, which include production designs, storyboards, and other materials. The design of stylish films is becoming a more recognized artistic discipline and is being refined. This leads to more highbrow "art-house" cinema with no point, and even larger audiences who arrogantly claim to understand exactly what the point is. But even if the majority of artistic films make use of this substance-free style poorly, and most pretentious indie audiences insist that the emperor is fully clothed, the growing mainstream popularity will only make film study materials more readily available.

The advent of the MTV style of storytelling has widened the cinematic vocabulary of audiences, but narrowed their real understanding. Many of the more original music video directors were later hired to craft style-heavy, substance-light films, and so today many of the more popular art-house directors will direct music videos for more "freedom of expression." As the Hollywood saying goes, "Make commercials for money, films for glory, and music videos for fun."

Which brings me back to the main point. This style-savvy and content-ignorant brand of mainstream filmmaking results in Hollywood's continuing to make films that don't make money, music videos that aren't glorious, and commercials that aren't any fun. As John Simon wrote, "Once a form has shown itself capable of great things, why settle for lesser ones?"

Film is a tool that has been used in a variety of ways and is being destroyed by the forces that are misusing it today. Nevertheless, its potential is enormous. It needs new professionals who are serious about professionalism, yet not dependent on the old routes that conformed film students to the Hollywood mindset or business structure. A biblically-minded, perceptive generation will be able to create films that prove that the medium is still capable of great things.

The final products of our creative labors must fulfill three criteria. They must be technically superior—not shoddy or imitative of current trends or gimmicks. Their content must be truthful—never contradicting Scripture or what is right. Their function must be noble—not degrading or manipulative.

Just as important as these are *how* we go about creating these works of art. We can't crawl to Hollywood and we can't mix their chaff in with the wheat. We must compare the quality of our work with what they do well—but we can't fight their fight on their turf. If we do that, we'll be sucked into their system and be victim to that system's complex political controls.

The new trends in filmmaking and film technology make a fruitful career in movies possible outside of Hollywood.

Go bear some fruit.

MOST COMMON MISTAKES OF BEGINNING DIRECTORS

WRONG CHOICE OF PROJECT

If a director works from a bad script or an incomplete script, his project is doomed to mediocrity at best. A weak premise will never lead to a strong script.

TOO LITTLE SUBTEXT

Scripts that have too little subtext need to be filled-in by the director with his interpretive vision. If the script is lean, and the director's own input doesn't round out what is necessary to make sense of the script, the finished product will be lame.

A script needs more information behind it than turns up in the spoken dialogue. The script needs subtext to explain the motivations of the actors and the backstory of the plot.

It can, however, have too much description on the script page; that makes for a heavy script that can be hard to read. It needs balanced subtext that covers all the aspects of a character or story point that need to end up on the screen. In order to do this, the writer needs to write even more data that will never make the screen *or* the script page.

JUMPING THE GUN

Too many directors stop rewriting at the fifth draft. A weak script may take many more to make it strong enough to justify beginning the shooting process. By not rewriting enough, some directors simply begin shooting too early. The biggest weakness in weak scripts is the ending. The ending *is* the story. Thus, a script with a weak ending means there's no story for the director to begin shooting on.

TOO MUCH DIRECTORIAL INFLUENCE

Small, low-budget projects are often hampered by a limited number of professional crew members, so the director will usually carry the film by wearing a number of different hats. This is usually good, both for the production and the finished product, and will only cause a problem if he tries to do more than he can physically manage, or more than he has the expertise to accomplish.

However, some new directors are ego-driven to be one-man bands, and end up being prima donnas on their own films, which usually end up produced by, written by, and starring the director, who is probably also the credited

composer, director of photography, and publicist. Any
project based solely on personal pride is doomed from the
start, and any project where the director refuses to accept
ideas from his crew is crippled.

NOT ENOUGH DIRECTORIAL CONTROL

To create a coherent feature film with a solid script and a
unified purpose, the crew needs share a common goal and
understand a single vision. It is the job of the director to
develop and communicate this vision to the crew and the
audience. The director needs to plan out all the elements of
the film and how they all contribute to a single story.

In the early days of the studios, executives would hire
authors to write scripts. The script was finished when the
deadline was up, and the writer moved on to his next
project. The producers would then cast the film, and decide
on a director. They would also choose costume designers,
carpenters, cameramen, and lighting technicians based more
on availability than specific artistic strengths.

The director would work with all of these individuals
who had been hired by the studios, and shoot several reels
of film. The filming was finished when all the pages of the
script had been shot, and then the cast, crew, and director
all moved on to their next projects. The studio would
then assign an editor and composer to the film, and so the
director really only served as a glorified acting coach.

Some directors had a larger vision for their films, and wanted more power over the casting process, the art design, and, most importantly, the script and the editing. Important directors working on important films often got special favors and freedoms from the studios, but some directors had to be very innovative to make sure that their vision ended up in the final film.

John Ford was particularly clear in his mind as to how his films should be edited, but in his early days never had the authority to control the final cut, or even to be involved in the editorial process. He, got around this problem, as did his contemporaries John Huston and Alfred Hitchcock, by shooting from a strict storyboard and delivering only the bare minimum of shots needed to cut the film together. Studio editors had no choice but to assemble the film his way.

Many modern directors are lazily falling into the old studio work flow; delegating artistic decisions to department heads who have been chosen for their union qualifications rather than their compatibility with the director's over-arching vision for the entire film. The result is inevitably a patchwork muddle of disjointed elements compiled into a weak film without a cohesive purpose.

Sometimes this is due to the director not having a vision for the film, and sometimes it's due to his inability or cowardice in communicating that vision. Any director who isn't actively and intimately involved in the script, storyboards, art design, casting, camerawork, lighting, acting, editing, scoring, effects, and marketing is not driving the film.

A good leader will be able to create and communicate the unified message, purpose, and plan of the film, to all the members of his crew. If he does so properly, he won't be a tyrant of ideas, but will have inspired his employees with a vision that they can creatively contribute to in unity, rather than accidentally detract from.

A good director won't be afraid to tell his cameraman where to point the camera, his lighting engineers where to put the lights, and his composer what instruments to use. He'll hire creative professionals with great artistic ability and rely on their judgment for many things, but will always retain his position as the ultimate authority and the guardian of the film's unified message.

NO STORYBOARDING

Some directors show up on-set thinking they can create all the framing "on the fly." Finished scenes are unusable to the editor because they don't cut together in a coherent fashion. There may be enough coverage of the scene to make a complete film, but it won't have been planned out for the maximum effect.

BAD STORYBOARDING

Storyboards must track the way the mind thinks. This one is tricky to learn. I've worked at studios where the producer didn't understand this and simply hired the storyboard artist who drew the prettiest pictures. Unfortunately, the best artists often turned out to be poor storyboardists, simply because of inexperience. It takes awhile to learn, but the storyboard must cut together in a way that tells the story so that it follows the way an audience thinks.

Directors must learn to do this for themselves. A director who can't direct his films on paper will be useless on set, and a director who has delegated the storyboards to an artist, however talented, has surrendered his position as the visual director and is now merely an acting coach. Few directors can draw well, so most do thumbnail sketches of their boards using stick figures and then, if the budget allows and the crew is large enough to merit it, has a professional artist, usually already part of the art department, draw up cleaner and clearer boards.

CROSSED CENTER LINE FROM CUT TO CUT

This is another common problem I saw often on storyboards from artists who were illiterate in the grammar of filmmaking. Anything that takes place, from a conversation to a car chase or a gunfight, has a line of action. The camera must stay on the same line as that action, or the audience will be confused when the scene suddenly cuts, flipping the direction of the action. It's visually jarring and pulls the viewers out of the scene.

If two characters are talking, no matter how the camera moves, the one on the right must stay on the right, facing the left, and the one on the left must stay on the left, facing the right. Having the two suddenly swap places between cuts is startling. The "center line" can be understood as a "facing line." Which direction is the actor or the action facing? The line is sometimes known as the "nose line." In which direction is the actor's nose pointing? With every cut, the nose needs to keep pointing in that direction unless we see the nose move to the other direction in the same "take." It must not change direction in a cut. It must happen in the scene, on camera.

The center line can only be crossed if there is a new establishing shot which shows the new camera configuration, and a new establishing shot should only exist when something new needs to be established, such as a new character entering.

Fast action is harder to handle. If you're shooting a car chase, you may have the paths of the cars swerve back and forth and change directions several times, which is difficult to keep clear. The camera should keep the action moving from one side of the screen to the other, from left to right, or vice versa. If the cars turn to go the other way, the camera must show them driving left to right, then turning, and then driving right to left in a single take.

INSUFFICIENT OR LESS-THAN-COMPREHENSIVE REHEARSALS

Rehearsals exist to make the actual takes run smoother. If an actor is struggling to hit his marks, his performance will suffer. If a cameraman is having to react to an unexpected move from a crane operator, his framing will suffer. Rehearsals are vital for all members of the crew, but especially for actors.

A number of directors film their rehearsals to try and get a feeling of spontaneity, but very few actors can manage to hit their marks and remember their lines and interact and give a good performance without a walkthrough of what is required. Acting is a delicate balance between creative spontaneity and rigid adherence to the script and storyboard.

If an actor improvises too much of his own material into a take, there is no way of making sure that it will fit into the final vision of the film. However, if he simply reads his lines and walks from one mark to another in correct time, it's a very lifeless performance. A good actor will rehearse everything that he *must* do, and then use his own skill to be creative on top of that.

However, since the director is the only person on the set who has a complete idea of how every shot cuts together in his mind, he must give the actor good direction on how to play every line so that it matches up with the rest of the film. Rehearsals are usually the best place for the director to give line-by-line feedback and demonstrate what needs to be done.

Perhaps sometime in the future when everybody shoots with digital cameras straight to unlimited hard drives, it will be just as cheap to record all day as to record only selected takes. When that day comes, we can decide to just film all our rehearsals until they become takes, but for now nothing can beat limited resources like good planning and communication. Besides, too many takes complicates and extends the editing process.

MISMATCHED MOOD OR THEME LIGHTING

This seems like a small point, and in one respect it is, but lighting is a very powerful tool for communicating emotion, and it's a poor director who doesn't use all of his tools effectively. The director must be aware of the emotional subtext in the scene and match the lighting to it. Unique lighting for each character can reveal different things about each one. Study some of the films made by great cinematographers and watch how they use light. They have developed a vocabulary of moods and emotions using set colors and intensities that modern audiences subconsciously recognize and understand.

SATISFACTION WITH SUBSTANDARD TAKES

An inexperienced director usually has an incomplete idea of the final cut, and is unable to see how well each "take" fits into what he has in mind. Most new directors also believe that music and editing can punch up a take, which is true, but an unusable take remains an unusable take, regardless of much help it gets from post-production.

This inexperience also means that the director has a poor idea of how to communicate with his talent, and is usually uncomfortable asking for extra takes, even if it means a better result that would be a better use of his crew's time.

WEAK VISUAL ESTABLISHMENT OF NEW SCENES

It is important that the establishing shot contains all the information that the audience needs to see. Subconsciously, the viewer's brain can build a large map of where characters and props are on a set. What takes a paragraph or more in a novel can be easily done with a simple establishing shot at the beginning of a scene.

Say you have a diner filled with patrons. A good establishing shot should contain all the key elements of that scene. Anyone who speaks or plays any part in the scene should be in the establishing shot. If you need to introduce a new character halfway through the scene, it's stronger if we see him enter the diner, and not just suddenly appear from offscreen, where he's been all along.

And like the director who uses lighting to communicate a mood, use this shot to establish a mood as well. It's the beginning of a scene, and the audience will be scanning it for clues. Manage the camera angle, placement of props, lighting, etc. to make sure that the tone of the scene is matched by its establishing shot.

FEAR OF USING THE WIDE SHOT OR THE CLOSE-UP

Years ago, the trend for student films was to keep the camera far from the actors and shoot lengthy takes of action. Today's inexperienced directors tend to rely more on extreme close-ups and fast cuts. Using the former style too much makes for a slow-moving film that lacks intimacy, and over-using the latter can result in sporadic confusion.

The balance between these types of shots is different for every film and every scene. A good director works that balance out ahead of time with the storyboard and tweaks it in editing. When the audience wants to see what's going on in the whole scene, they should be given a wide shot. When they want to see emotion, they should be given close-ups. Of course, these rules exist to be broken, but *only* if you know what you are a doing. A good director will not rely too heavily on one type of shot simply because he is personally more comfortable with it.

MISMANAGEMENT OF LOGISTICS AND BUDGET

This sounds obvious, and it really should be. But too many projects are never completed, either because the initial budget was incorrect or it was not followed. If the smallest responsibility is dropped by the most insignificant crewmember, the effort required to correct that mistake could cause the whole production to fall over. The director and producer are responsible to see to it that every person performs every assigned task completely and on time.

The schedule is just as important as the budget. Obviously, the schedule needs to be realistic, like the budget, and sticking to it will ensure that all the aspects of production have the time, as well as the resources, to create the best results.

Appendix B.

EQUIPMENT

This is a difficult appendix to write. If I've communicated the principles in this book well, it should be easy to see that they aren't my ideas as much as principles from God's word and the testimony of history. These ideas are timeless.

By contrast, any equipment recommendations will be utterly obsolete before the ink on this page has dried. However, by this point you should have a pretty good idea of the technical basics required for all the types of productions described so far, so you'll be able to do a lot of the research on your own. If you know what you need to make, you can work backwards from there and figure out what you need. Also, take a look at **www.outside-hollywood.com** for more recent info. Following are some basics that should get you started....

A good gear wholesaler is B&H Photo and Video in New York. They carry a full range of new and used gear, from 35mm cameras to mini-video camera tripods. They've got lights, teleprompters, computer software, and staff that are well-informed and helpful. You can ask them questions about the up-to-date equipment, and they can give you good prices on the used stuff.

But really, you are mostly on your own for research, since you are the only person that knows your exact needs. Try to find all the technical specs on the Web for any gear that you're looking at, and see if you can find other people who use it. Ask them how well it works, or even how it works. Most importantly, find out the requirements for the type of product you will be creating and work backwards from there.

For example, broadcast-quality, D1 NTSC video is 720 pixels by 486 pixels. It runs at 29.97 frames per second, with two fields per frame. There are far more detailed requirements for audio, but most SD broadcasters (at the writing of this book) will ask for a DigiBeta master with D1 video at specific levels and two or four channels of audio. DVD duplication houses will have slightly different requirements.

If you know what you need to make, you can work backwards from there and figure out what you need. Here are some basics that should get you started....

CAMERAS

The most exciting development in the past few years has been the development of digital cameras and the DV formats. Now you can get a consumer camera with the same MiniDV tape deck as a professional news camera, and it uses the same "FireWire" port to communicate that data to another edit deck or a computer.

The advantage of this system is that the video is digitally compressed by the camera itself, so a full resolution frame is captured. This compressed signal can be directly accessed by a computer plugged into the camera by a FireWire cable. The disadvantage is that the DV signal is very compressed. This means that a lot of the detail is averaged, approximated, and simplified into an image with less clarity.

Most top-level production will still be done using more expensive gear with uncompressed video, but the DV family (DV, DVCpro, MiniDV) is compressed. Is it acceptable? That is up to the end-user. Find out as much about the end-user of your productions before you buy. As you shop, keep recording quality in mind also. The camera's lens and CCD chip must be of good quality to shoot superior images. Make sure you research the camera's lens array and try to get a camera with three separate ⅔" CCDs.

But that's only for standard definition (SD) DV cameras. The rules are changing rapidly with the implementation of HD broadcast channels and the development of new HD technologies. Each manufacturer is taking a different route in creating their new HD cameras, and each unit has certain features and prices that make them better for different circumstances.

However, Sony does generally make the better cameras, closely followed by Canon, JVC, and Panasonic. Canon and Fuji make the best lenses. Each camera is also taking a different approach to the HD formats. At present there are two main HD standards; 1080i, which is 1920x1080 and 30 frames (interlaced 60 fields) per second, and 720p, which is 1280x720 and 60 progressive frames per second.

These two formats are very similar in terms of bandwidth requirements and can be converted back and forth with relative ease using professional conversion tools. However, there is great debate over which is the superior standard, largely due to a lack of truly standards-compatible HD televisions. Some lack the speed for 720p's progressive frames, and interlace them. Others don't have the resolution for full 1080i, and downsample it to something closer to a 720 pixel height.

At present, only professional equipment is really capable of creating and viewing the two HD formats properly, but there are some new displays and cameras that come very close to replicating the precision of the more expensive studio gear. Much in line with the advance of DV is the HDV format, which promises true HD video from a small DV-style camera. There are HDV formats for both 720p and 1080i, but not all HDV cameras support both standards.

At the time of this writing, there are several HDV camcorders on the market. Each is small and light, and most seem to be having a few teething problems. Some of these problems seem to be related to the new, untested chipsets used by these cameras, and some are related to the HDV format itself. HDV uses the same MiniDV tapes running at the same speed (and thus, same bitrate) as other DV cameras, but manages to pack six times the number of pixels. This means six times the compression.

It's more complicated than that, though. HDV uses a more efficient version of the MPEG2 codec to create an image that is not six times worse than DV's already-ugly compression. Part of this efficiency is achieved by sharing image data across multiple frames. This is called "Long-GOP" encoding, and it enables a much larger and crisper image to be stored in a smaller space.

Unfortunately, this makes editing much harder. Because frames are made up of data stored across a set of up to 15 other frames, half a second of video must be decoded to pick out a single frame. If any cuts are to be made within that 15-frame chunk, the two clips on either side of the edit will need to be re-encoded. There are several HDV editing plugins for most mainstream editing programs which help to streamline these difficulties, but it is still an awkward format.

And despite the greater efficiency of the codec, the quality of the HDV image is still very low. Compression artifacts are more obvious than on DV, there is less color information, and fast motion can confuse the multi-frame long-GOP system. For now, many networks, such as the BBC, have declared that HDV is not broadcast-quality. However, some of the issues may be addressed with later versions of the HDV system, or in HDV's successor.

The development of tools for HD creation will also be governed by various HD outlets, all of which are still growing, some of which are still being created. The transition from broadcast SD to broadcast HD will likely be similar in speed to the change-over from black and white to color television.

However, more interesting to the filmmaker is the fact that 1080i's 1920x1080 resolution is only somewhat smaller than a 2K film image, usually scanned at 2048x1556. HDCAM is HDV's bigger, older brother, which can capture images with far better quality and depth. Newer HDCAM cameras also have the ability to run at 24 frames per second. True 24p video doesn't play natively on most regular or even many HD televisions, but it's required for any footage that will be printed onto film for theatrical distribution.

The equipment needed to record and play uncompressed (or even slightly compressed) HDCAM video is extremely expensive, and it still lacks most of the resolution and dynamic depth of film. However, it's close enough for many feature projects. Far more complex digital-film solutions are being created, but as more and more television channels switch to HD, and a standard for HD-capable DVDs is settled on, there will be new HD production tools for smaller studios.

Some of these newer HD solutions will be perfectly adequate for smaller feature productions, and cheap enough for start-up studios and filmmakers to purchase on their own. However, this vision might be a little ambitious and is certainly only an optimistic guess. You may need to start off practicing your storytelling technique with smaller-scale SD TV gear, but don't hesitate to think big. Research big.

No matter what cameras look like by the time you start researching, these are some things to look for. Interchangeable lenses: even if you buy only one lens, it's handy to have the ability to rent another and use it on your own camera. You should also have video out, so you can see the camera's output on a field monitor as you shoot. Manual settings: check that you have manual focus, manual iris, manual shutter speed, and manual white balance. Manual settings will get better results and teach you more about shooting. When you move up to film or digital cinema, the cameras are entirely manual.

You will also want three CCDs, since one CCD captures a grainier image. CMOS sensors tend to have shutter problems. You should have a way of setting your own timecode on your tapes, regardless of what kind of tape it is. If it is a digital camera, you should have some way of getting a digital feed from it directly into your computer. Also, you will need multiple microphone inputs, both "line" and "mic" level options, and they should have their own volume settings and visual meters. I'm not certain that you will always be able get all of these features on a reasonable priced camera, but they are important, so work backwards and decide what you can do without.

MISCELLANEOUS GEAR

No matter how big or small your initial projects are, you will still need some of the basics. Your camera will need a solid tripod. It needs to be sturdy enough to be stable, but light enough that you can carry it a long way (which, inevitably, you will). The tripod needs a smooth head; something that will let you pan and tilt without sticking or needing to be forced.

You will also, eventually, need lights. Your lighting setup will be dictated entirely by what you are filming. Ambush-style interviews might need a small light on the top of the camera (called a "sun gun"). Sit-down interviews should have a basic three-point lighting setup. Outdoor shots may look great with no more than one reflector. Massive, dramatic film scenes sometimes need trucks full of lighting gear. Be flexible.

Sound gear is equally tricky to recommend; simple in-camera stuff can often get by with a camera-mounted shotgun mic – but not the cheap stereo one that comes with the camera. An interview will require a lapel mic on the interviewee's chest. If you are using an external mic, see if your camera will let you record it to audio channel one, and set the camera-mounted mic to channel two. A good camera will let you do this, and if you're in a changing environment, you could set the camera mic to "auto" and leave the lapel on manual (after a soundcheck).

Film set sound is a different beast; few people record the final dialog to film, since few cinema cameras have any audio components. Most productions have a dedicated audio mixer who records the sound on his own gear. He usually has an assistant with a boom microphone who stays close to the action. He may also have small radio microphones on the actors which he also controls. He will record all the channels separately for more freedom in the final mix.

COMPUTER HARDWARE

The main decision to be made will be between PC and Mac. At the time of this writing, Apple is trying to take over the low-end video production market. In the late eighties and early nineties, the Macintosh computer ruled the print media industry with Photoshop and Quark running exclusively on Apple hardware. IBM and Tandy computers running DOS could not compete with its advanced graphics capabilities. Apple wants those days of market domination back.

Today, however, things are different; Apple has switched to Intel processors, and the new Macintosh "media" machines are running the identical CPUs and chip controllers that their cheaper Dell competitors contain. The new Macs roll off the same production lines in the same

Chinese factories as Hewlett-Packards and Sony VAIOs.

The only differences in hardware are cosmetic, and the operating systems are beginning to mimic each other as well. However, the PC, running either Windows or Linux, dominates the professional film and television industry. No matter how much headway Apple makes in the industrial video production and indie hobbyist market, the vast majority of professional media companies, studios, and projects are powered by Windows workstations and servers.

Obviously, I'd like for the readers of this book to set their sights a little higher than the hobbyists. If it is best, for learning purposes, to buy a simple video editing appliance to hone storytelling skills, a Mac will fill the bill admirably, and may have several advantages. However, to better understand more areas of film, and learn computing skills that will be more useful on larger projects, many readers should look into PCs.

The PC accommodates a wider array of software, gets hardware upgrades sooner, and is usually much cheaper. For animation work, the best approach is to get a number of fast, cheap computers to handle the rendering while you are animating. With processor speeds constantly climbing and RAM prices dropping, PCs offer the best power-per-dollar ratio, and far more upgrade and expansion options.

As far as operating systems go, you're pretty much stuck with OS X or Windows. While Linux is cheaper, more stable, and more powerful, it is only the extreme high-end of the specialty pro software that is designed to run on Linux, Unix, or Irix, and they usually require expensive extra hardware. Almost all of the applications available for entry-level video and effects work are available for Windows, and so are most of the top-level professional post-production programs.

EDITING SOFTWARE

Editing was invented on the first films; the editor would physically cut the strips of film and stick them back together with cellophane tape or rubber cement. Some films are still edited this way. When video tape was invented in the late '70s, it was edited using two tape decks, one playing the video signal and the other recording it onto the master tape. This required the editor to work in a linear way, from the start of the tape to the end, like writing a letter on a typewriter.

With the advent of computer technology that could digitize footage, a new, non-linear style of editing was invented. It's almost as easy as editing a letter in a word processor. Individual clips can be chopped up and dragged around on a timeline along with music underneath and transparent graphics on the top. It's a revolutionary concept for editing, and the first company to build a non-linear editor was Avid.

Avid's first systems were a combination of special software and expensive hardware (even for just storing the huge video files), but today's computers are capable of digitizing and storing video data right out of the box, and most editing packages are only editing software. However, certain hardware cards offer extra input formats or certain real-time transitions and effects.

But it's the software that's the important part. **Avid** still sells a number of different editing packages, each designed for a different market. They have them for high-speed news editing, long-form feature film editing, basic video production, and cheaper learning editions for film and broadcast schools – even a free version that you can download from their website. At the time of this writing, it is estimated that Avid software is used for 90% of all professional video and television projects, and 80% of all feature films (the remainder use even more expensive programs like **Lightworks**).

Apple provides simple yet powerful editing software which is growing in popularity among independent film groupies. **Final Cut Pro** is a solid editing package. It is available in the Final Cut Studio package, which includes programs for creating with graphics, working with music, and authoring DVDs, but is only available for Apple computers.

Adobe makes what is arguably a more widely-used program, called **Premiere Pro**. Premiere is also a great program for learning on, and it is most economical to purchase it in the Adobe Production Studio, which includes After Effects, Photoshop, and other software packages

for audio editing and DVD authoring. At the time of
this writing, these extra applications outclass their Apple
counterparts, and also provide a much more integrated
studio package. By the time you read this, all the programs
in the bundle should be available for Windows and OS X,
and so this is my own personal recommendation for those
who want a complete studio in a box but don't feel that they
will require all the upgradeable firepower of Avid.

However, neither Premiere nor Final Cut Pro, which were
both designed by Randy Ubillos and are, in essence, the
same program, would be the first choice of a professional,
full-time editor. There are numerous top-dollar editing suites
in addition to Avid's turnkey systems which offer special
features and special uses that are arguably much better
programs for certain projects.

There are also several much cheaper programs, like
Sony's **Vegas**, or Avid's consumer program **Pinnacle Studio**.
Limited editing can also be done on Apple's **iMovie** and
Microsoft's **MovieMaker**, both of which come free with
their respective operating systems. All of these programs
can be used for capturing and rearranging video clips, but
the professional Apple and Adobe software will do so in a
more streamlined manner with more features, and the more
expensive programs add even more speed and functionality
to those.

However, learning to edit is like learning to write. Once
you know how to write, it's pretty easy to use any word

processor to craft a letter or a book. It's the technique of visual storytelling that needs to be learned to master the craft of editing, and the cheaper programs may be fine for that.

COMPOSITING AND GRAPHICS SOFTWARE

For some animation and logo work, the best tools will be video compositing programs. They'll offer more graphical control than a non-linear editor, and can be used for a number of effects. Originally designed for blue-screen compositing, they are now capable of manipulating any digitized video in almost any way.

Top of the heap for actual visual effects work is Digital Domain's **Nuke**, one of the first super-powered film compositing packages developed by a major visual effects studio to be released for off-the-shelf sales. It excels in all kinds of post work, but probably isn't anyone's first choice for making simpler graphics like DVD menus.

Next is probably **Quantel**'s linup, which includes everything from dedicated film coloring systems to real-time broadcast graphics stations. Another industry leader is **Autodesk**, formerly Discreet, who create the **Flint**, **Flame**, and other high-powered compositing programs, as well as the much cheaper **Combustion** and **Toxik**, which have many industrial-strength color correction and keying tools.

Then there are Interactive Effects' very successful **Piranha** compositing and **Amazon** paint systems, which are popular choices for animation studios like Pixar, Dreamworks, and PDI.

Any of the above programs would be ubiquitous to the post production process of any major studio film or big-budget television commercial, but they are all very expensive to purchase. A cheaper option is eyeon's **Digital Fusion** which originally had a slightly confusing interface reminiscent of the workflow of a genuine optical printer, but it has developed into a very powerful node-based compositor with many features.

A former industry leader is **Shake**, which was purchased by Apple at the height of its success, but dwindled in popularity as development stalled, and now that the product itself has been cancelled, its future is uncertain. Licenses of Shake can be purchased very cheaply (for Mac), but there is no product support available, and there will be no future upgrades. Much of the Shake code is rumored to be incorporated into a new Apple graphics package, but is becoming clear that it only select features are being absorbed by Motion and Final Cut.

What might be more useful to readers is Adobe's **After Effects**, which ties directly into Premiere and Photoshop. It has a similar workflow and interface between those two applications, and shares a number of assets and effects, making it very easy to learn. It is commonly used for broadcast graphics and effects, but with a number of plug-ins that emulate the features of more expensive programs, is regularly used on many large and small 35mm feature projects, often as a primary post tool.

3D ANIMATION SOFTWARE

The top of the heap for 3D software is definitely **Maya**. Originally created by SGI in association with George Lucas's ILM, it is the high-powered, big dollar package that is used for most of the high-profile computer graphics that you'll see today. But a free, scaled-down learning package is available from their web site. Prices on it change drastically from month to year, and certain educational deals may be found. Recommended, but beware—the learning curve is brutal. Main strengths: Character animation, customizability, and sheer market saturation.

Next on the list, in terms of prominence and big-studio-power, is **Softimage**. Softimage was the original leader of the pack, but after it was purchased by Microsoft, it was very poorly represented, lost its hold, and is no longer top dog. It has been sold to Avid, who is doing a much better job of developing it for the market, but it will probably never take back the lead it lost to Maya. Examine carefully. Main strengths: Organic effects and facial animation.

Third on the list is **Lightwave**, which is what I learned on. It lacks the power of Maya in some areas, but it has a superior, rock-solid rendering engine. It began on the Amiga as the industry-standard tool for FX work on episodic television programs, and has since moved up to a lot of feature work. It is advancing well and has potential to grow much further. Main strengths: Vehicles, effects, realistic renders, and raw speed.

Next is **3D Studio Max**. 3DS started off as the only real PC-based, entry-level 3D program, and got a strong hold on the independent video producers, game authors, and Web designers. It is still a strong player, even though it offers very few groundbreaking capabilities in any area. It has a background in CAD design and architectural schematic work. Main strengths: Architecture and logos.

At the bottom of the list are low-end packages, such as Strata Studio, Cinema 4D, formZ, Animation Master, Carrara, and others, which are cheap and sometimes even free on the CDs that come with computer magazines. Pretty much unable to integrate with the big programs, and also unable to create really good realistic photoreal content, they do have for basic logo-type stuff. Probably somewhat useful for learning very basic principles, they could also teach very bad habits.

Outside of the list, but still something to be aware of, are also several **high-end packages** for specific work. For example, Houdini, a very powerful particle-based animation system for fire, water, and other super-complex work at the film level. Also, Pixar's Renderman, which is often used to replace Maya's sub-par renderer. Certain Renderman-based rendering engines are available for all flavors of Unix and Linux for render farms of massive computer banks.

Of course, most major studios also have **proprietary tools**, such as the Massive crowd animation system that Weta Digital developed for *The Lord of the Rings* or the specialized facial animation systems used by Pixar. Often an effects-heavy feature film with a lot of complicated 3D will result in a number of special tools being written. Some will be kept under wraps by the effects company for later use, but under certain circumstances, proprietary tools will appear on the market later as plugins.

Plugins are small software tools that "plug in" to another 3D program to give it extra capabilities. Almost every different package has a different set of plugins that are made to handle fire, water, cloth, fur, crowd simulations, lip-sync, and/or anything else that the original application may not do too well. Some plugins are specific to a certain program and others can be interface with most of the major applications. Some plugins change the look of the final render to look like cartoon artwork.

2D ANIMATION

It's hard to recommend 2D tools for the independent filmmaker, because 2D animation is so labor-intensive that it generally takes a small army of animators to get the most out of any professional software. It is also pretty expensive. Nevertheless, the best of these will probably be represented by the **Animo** system. They offer a pretty flexible scheme for different needs. Next up is **Toon Boom**. I haven't looked at them in a while, but they have a solid system as well.

The prevalence of Asian animated shows and animation studios has fueled the expansion of a few more packages, most notably **Bauhaus Mirage**, and the modular pick-and-choose **Retas** system. These are both fully-featured and flexible enough to be applicable for feature films or Saturday-morning cartoons.

However, for simply learning the basics of 2D Disney-style hand-drawn animation, I recommend Adobe **Flash,** which now comes bundles with Adobe's video production package. It might be difficult to use for some tasks, but it has all the tools that an animator needs to draw simple frame-by-frame motion. It is best when coupled with a tablet and the animator can draw right into the program.

If you already have finished animation, created either on paper or in Flash, you can take the frames into Adobe **Photoshop** to be painted, and then composite them over backgrounds using any of the compositing programs listed above. Obviously, if you can work entirely whithin Adobe products, the process is much more streamlined. This isn't quite as elegant as a dedicated 2D ink-and-paint and layout program, but it will be far cheaper for smaller projects.

Unfortunately, there isn't currently much of a market for 2D animators or 2D animated films. Fox's 2D animation studio was shut down after two or three films, Dreamworks shut theirs down after three films, and *Home on the Range* was Disney's last 2D film until Pixar can rebuild their 2D department (which they are doing with off-the-shelf software). 3D films are cheaper and have had better box office returns than their 2D counterparts. It is my belief that this is because the 3D films have, so far, simply been more compelling movies than Disney's latest 2D projects.

This said, 2D animation is very useful for learning strong character animation technique. A 2D animator with good, strong character work on his demo reel will be hired to work at a 3D studio over a 3D artist with poor, basic skills. Bear in mind that our main goal must be to become writers, directors, and producers—but animation is good groundwork for learning principles. However, it can be time-consuming to master animation enough to begin to learn film, so examine all your options wisely.

Appendix C.

GLOSSARY

A-B Roll Editing: The original method of video editing; using three tape-based video machines, two playing, one recording, to record only the scenes wanted onto a final master tape. This type of editing must be done from start to finish in a linear fashion, with cuts or dissolves between each different visual. Sometimes referred to as "assemble editing."

ADR (additional dialogue recording): If for any reason the audio recorded on-set is unusable, the actor involved will be called back to record new dialogue that will sync directly with his mouth movements from the footage. Because he will watch a shot over and over to memorize the timing and inflection, this is sometimes called "looping in dialogue."

Ambiance: A scene's mood, or feeling. Generally generated by things that are ambient to the main characters, dialogue, or action. Elements contributing to it would include music, lighting, sound effects, set design, and subtle camera work.

Antagonist: The character whose total objective is to stop the protagonist from reaching his ultimate goal.

Art Director: The Art Director is responsible for coordinating the stylistic consistency of all the artistic elements in a production. This includes the construction of the sets, the design of the costumes, and the types of props. Advanced Art Directors also factor-in lighting, film stock, actor enculturation, and camera-mounts. He must convey the Director's general artistic ideas to the technicians and make sure there is continuity between all their efforts.

Aspect Ratio: How wide the screen is compared to how tall it is. Television is 4:3, most films are shot in "academy" ratio, which is 1.33:1, and is usually masked down to a wider ratio. HDTV is 16:9, as are most widescreen DVD presentations.

Assistant Cameraman: Responsible for loading and unloading the camera, protecting the film stock from the elements, lens changes, keeping camera reports on takes and film used, and in general assisting the Operator. Also usually marks out the focus distances prior to takes.

Assistant Director: There can be several assistant directors, but the First AD is the Director's right-hand man. He works on the set, supervising the actions of the talent, staff, and keeps track of the production schedule. If filming large crowd scenes, the Director will focus on the main actors, and the AD will relay orders to the extras with a megaphone.

The AD helps do the Director's smaller jobs so he can focus on more important things.

AVI: (Audio-Video Interleave) the most common video format for Windows. It is simply a file type that is recognized as a "wrapper" containing video and audio information. That data streams contained within the avi "wrapper" can be digitized in almost any codec, DV included. It is similar to Apple's QuickTime file type.

Avid: The company that developed the first computer-based, non-linear editing system and still builds most of the high-end professional systems. Some directors will refer to any non-linear edit suite as "the Avid," in the same way photographers used to refer to all still cameras as "Kodaks."

Backstory: The contributing factors to any character's current position and attitude. Everything that has taken place before the events of the story.

Beat Sheet: A list of high and low points in a script. Usually a breakdown of key moments throughout the scenes, which can be used to plot the hero's journey and the basic story arc.

Beat: A plot point within the story structure, *or* a pause in an actor's delivery which adds to his performance.

Barn Doors: The metal folding doors on the four sides of most film and television lights. They can swing open and shut to control where the light falls on the set. Colored gels and diffusion can be clipped to the barn doors.

Best Boy: Assistant Gaffer or the assistant to the Key Grip. Usually responsible for the rigging and coiling of power cables for lights and other gear. Handles the purely technical, non-artistic side of lighting.

Beta: 1/2 inch videotape format developed by Sony in the 1970s. Originally called Betamax, it was defeated by the inferior VHS format for the home videocassette market. Sony then upgraded Beta to become the BetaCam format for use in top-level broadcast cameras. It has since been updated to the BetaSP and more lately DigiBeta formats and standards. It is gradually losing its hold to the cheaper DV formats in terms of television production, but DigiBeta still produces better broadcast-quality images. Sony has dropped the "Beta" name for its newer HDCAM tape format.

Blocking: Arranging the gear on a set so that filming is ready to begin by the time the talent arrives. Usually most of the work involves the lighting of the set, the placement of the camera for the shots needed, and the use of stand-ins to mark places for the actors to use later.

Blue Screen: A wall of a constant color used on TV or film sets to create images to be later composited with other images. By standing in front of the wall, actors or journalists can become foreground images that can be later, or even in real time, be combined with a different background. Blue is most commonly used because it contrasts with normal skin tones, but if special film stocks or blue costumes demand a different color, a green screen sometimes works better. Used for special effects and compositing. Green should also be used by filmmakers shooting on most digital video formats.

Blu-ray Disc: An optical disc developed by Sony and supported by a number of other manufacturers including Dell and Panasonic. It can hold 50 gigabytes of data on two layers, 100 gigabytes on four layers, and supports a maximum data transfer rate of 54 megabits per second at 1x speed. At the time of this writing, Blu-ray film releases are available from more studios than HD DVD.

Boom: The long pole that the microphone hangs from. The boom operator (or "boom thrower") tries to keep the microphone as close to the actors as possible and out of camera shot.

Bounce Card: Or Reflector. A silver or white board that light is bounced off of to highlight a certain area of the subject. Sometimes when filming outdoors a gold or bronze board or sheet will be used to offset the blueish light of the sun and sky.

Bracketing: Shooting a scene several times with different iris and camera settings to experiment with the different settings and film stocks. A good Director of Photography will do this before filming begins, or know already how do achieve the effect he wants; an inexperienced one will have to bracket during filming to get the feel he is looking for.

CCD (Charged-Couple Device): The visual pickups used in most modern video cameras. Older cameras used a heavy image pickup tube that was so sensitive that it could be burned by bright light. CCDs are the much tougher light-sensitive computer chips that convert an image into data. The two most common sizes are 1/3" and 2/3" chips, the latter being better. Higher-quality cameras will also have three CCD chips capturing the red, green, and blue data separately for a much clearer image.

C-Stand: A sturdy, three-legged light stand with swinging, rather than folding legs. Able to accommodate heavy lights and a long arm that can hold flags or gobos.

Call Sheet: A list of every department's responsibilities on a certain date, letting them know when and where they are supposed to be for certain scenes. Call sheets should be finalized at least a week in advance.

Camera Reports: A written record of film stock usage: how much was delivered on set, how much was exposed, the condition of leftover reels, which "takes" were successful (and worth printing), any special instructions for the lab, and where in the script this film goes, so the editor can keep the final prints organized.

Character Arc: The development and change of a character over the course of the story. The rise and fall and rise of the protagonist can be charted by following his emotional position between plot points as it relates to his struggle to achieve his goals.

Clapper: The two sticks on the top of the slate that are slapped together to mark the beginning of a "take," providing a visual and audio reference point for editing purposes. The "clap" is seen and heard on one frame. Picture and audio are then synced to this frame. The clapper also refers to the person who marks the slate and holds it up in view of the camera prior to each "take." This person is often the Camera Assistant, who is sometimes called a "Clapper/ Loader." The "slate" is the part of the clapper on which is written reference information for the editor (name of production, DP, director, scene number, and take number.)

CMOS (Complementary Metal-Oxide-Semiconductor): A cheaper type of mass-manufactured image sensor than traditional CCDs, the CMOS sensor was originally used for simple, low-power applications like miniaturized cell phone cameras. However, CMOS technology has improved considerably, and several consumer video cameras now use single or multiple CMOS imaging chips. Despite great advances in resolution and color response, they are still inferior to CCD chips, particularly in low-light conditions, and have problems with a "rolling shutter."

Codec: The mathematical algorithm used to *compress* ("co") and *decompress* ("dec") digital video. There are a wide variety, all of which have different strengths and weaknesses. Not all codecs are suitable for broadcast-quality video, but there are several versions of the official DV codec that are acceptable. The same compression techniques can often be used on different computers with different software and even different file formats.

Color Bars: The test pattern that should be at the beginning of all analog videotapes. This enables proper adjustment and calibration to be made of the playback gear to the proper color references. The bars should be accompanied by a calibration audio tone so that audio levels can also be set. Most video cameras supply both of these signals at the touch of a button. Engineers prefer cameramen to give them thirty seconds of "bars and tone."

Color Correction: The process of adjusting the final print so that colors from shot to shot match even if shot on different film or under different lights. Today, color correction can refer to adjustments that are far more dramatic, like the desaturation in *Saving Private Ryan*, or the color "sweetening" in *Lord of the Rings.* The first devices developed to adjust specific color ranges were made by da Vinci, so directors often refer to any color manipulations as being made by "the da Vinci" regardless of what software or hardware is used. Video color correction can be done with virtually any editing or compositing program.

Color Temperature: A somewhat confusing method for specifying the color of a light source, regardless of its intensity. It is measured in degrees Kelvin, with higher numbers indicating bluer light and lower numbers indicating more yellow light. Daylight will be approximately 5500-5000K, fluorescent tubes about 4100K, and incandescent, tungsten-based lights as low as 2800K. Different film emulsions are designed to respond to different color temperatures, and should be selected and processed according to the varying conditions on different film sets. Video cameras compensate for differing color temperatures by performing a "white balance" to get a neutral color reference.

Continuity: In any one scene, different camera angles and different "takes" are required until the scene is completed. Often the takes are shot out of sequence in the script for reasons of convenience and are edited together later. "Continuity" refers to the person on set whose job it is to make sure that no visual discrepancies appear in the frame from shot to shot. Generally, it is one or two people with clipboards and Polaroid cameras assigned to watch for any mistakes that might turn up. They make sure that coats are not unbuttoned between takes, that food on plates isn't disturbed, or that levels of drinks in glasses proceed from full to empty as time passes. They also help remind costume and makeup departments how beat-up or disheveled actors should be for certain scenes.

Coverage: Coverage generally refers to whether or not a scene has been "covered" enough that it can be cut together in the editing room. Full coverage requires close-ups, establishing shots, cutaways: everything that can be assembled into a finished scene. Good directors have the scene already storyboarded, either on paper or in their heads, so they know exactly which shots they need to completely "cover" the scene.

Dailies: After a day's shooting, the film is sent to the lab for processing overnight, and it comes back for the director to watch the next morning. These dailies let him check to see if any of the previous day's scenes need to be re-shot, and just how the film is coming along. On video shoots, the tape can be rewound and viewed instantly, so dailies might refer to scenes that the editor has cut together during the night. Also known as "rushes."

Dialogue Pass: The rewrite where the writer focuses only on the dialogue in a script. Other drafts might specifically polish plot, story, or subtext, but the dialogue pass is generally one of the later, final stages.

Diffusion: Translucent material such as spun cotton, lace, silk, or paper that is hung in front of a light to soften its shadows. It creates diffused, indirect lighting. Sometimes for outdoor sets, a large silk sail will be stretched and a battery of lights directed at it to give off soft, even light across a large area.

Dimmer Board: A switchboard for the electrical system that the lights are plugged into, which has a dimmer switch for each light, allowing the lighting team to control them very effectively. More common on indoor sets and sound stages than on location.

Director of Photography: Also known as the "DP" or the "Cinematographer." Helps to translate the director's idea for each shot into an equipment list and detailed instructions for the camera and lighting teams. He also controls the camera settings, decides which film stocks should be used, and has a hand in the setting used to develop the film later. The DP often is the camera operator as well.

Development: The process of crafting an idea into a script or a completed script into a shooting script, ready for production.

Development Hell: Slang for the negotiating period of conforming creative projects to Hollywood standards of political correctness, unreasonable legal requirements, and immature personal demands. Some scripts spend years stuck in development hell before it is even decided if they will be made or not.

Dolly: A wheeled camera-mount that is designed to move the camera smoothly. Most dollies carry the camera and cameraman, are pushed by hand, and run on tracks laid earlier by grips. Some have large pneumatic tires for use outside, and these are generally called "western dollies" and are rolled over sheets of plywood. Wheelchairs, skateboards, and shopping carts have been used by desperate directors in low-budget circumstances, however, the greater weight of a professional dolly will give a smoother, inertia-damped ride.

Dolly Shot: Almost any shot in which the camera is moving. Usually the dolly moves forward or backwards from the camera's perspective. A shot in which the camera moves left or right is usually called a "trucking" shot. In a "crane" shot the camera moves up and down. Some elaborate dollies have crane booms and curved dolly tracks and combine all three moves in one take.

Dressing: The action of preparing a set for shooting. A set-dresser will make the set looked "lived in," filling it with props and clutter and adding to its appearance of authenticity.

DV: The most common video format in use today, used by professionals and consumers alike. The cameras digitize video with the MJPEG-based DV codec at 25 megabits per second and write it directly to tape as compressed digital data. This data can be converted to analog video or copied to a computer over a dedicated data connection. The most common tape formats are DVCAM or MiniDV. Panasonic has also created DVCPRO and DVCPRO50 formats, the latter of which runs the tape faster to achieve twice the quality at 50 megabits per second.

DVD: A high-density optical disc format developed in 1995 for storing data and digital video. It can hold 9.4 gigabytes of data on two layers, and supports a maximum data transfer rate of 11 megabits per second at 1x speed. The DVD-Video standard specification ensures compatibility with set-top DVD players and specifies MPEG-2 video files and Dolby or PCM audio files in a specific directory structure.

Editor: The Editor is directly responsible to the Director and assembles all of the film shot into the final cut. Depending on the creative relationship between the director and the editor, the editor may be on set, making suggestions and attending screenings of dailies. The editor may help organize film rolls with the laboratory and will supply any material that is needed, such as looping strips for ADR sessions.

F-Stop: The units marked on the lens used to measure the size of the iris, which controls how much light hits the film. The larger the number, the smaller the iris opening, and less light is let in. The F-stops marked on most lenses are 1.4, 2, 2.8, 4, 5.6, 8, 11, 16, and 22.

Feature: A full-length dramatic movie, usually from 90 to 120 minutes in length.

Fields: The way that a television creates its image involves the cathode ray scanning from top to bottom. Video frame rates are 30 frames per second with NTSC and 25 fps with PAL. However, each of these frames is made up of two fields. The two fields are interlaced on alternating scanlines, which is done by first drawing one field consisting of an image's odd scan lines (1, 3, 5...) and then drawing the remaining even scan lines (2, 4, 6...) so that during playback the TV gives the impression of 60 fps (or 50). Film shoots full frames; it doesn't have fields or scanlines. DVDs are also usually non-interlaced. However, when film is broadcast on television, the non-interlaced frames of the 24fps film are spread across video fields in order to fit into the 30fps of NTSC video.

Filters: The film occasionally needs to be shot through glass filters tinted with different colors or densities to get the visual results on film the DP wants. The filters slot into the square "matte box" on the front of the camera lens. Some video lenses are made to accommodate filters, but these are usually to block light, correct color, and prevent "bloom." Most professional video cameras have three selectable filters built in, which are usually sufficient for field work.

Film Stock: Unprocessed film. Ordered by the DP, it arrives in rolls which are loaded into the camera magazines by the assistant cameraman. There are many different types and "speeds" of film, each of which must be understood by the DP in order to chose the right ones that will give him the final effect he is looking for under the circumstance in which he is filming.

FireWire: A high-speed digital connection interface, usually used to transfer video and audio data from a DV camera to a computer in real-time. This method of capturing digital video is lossless and can be done on nearly any modern computer without special video cards. Also known as IEEE-1394 and iLink.

Focal Length: Technically, the distance from the center of lens to the point at which the light rays meet in sharp focus. Essentially, how wide or narrow a lens focuses an image. A zoom lens sees a small field of view a long way off, a wide angle lens sees more of the scene close up. An extremely wide angle lens is known as a "fish-eye" lens, because its focal length is so wide that its view is distorted.

Focus Puller: The focus puller is usually the assistant cameraman and he adjusts the focus on the lens without taking the viewfinder away from the camera operator. With film cameras, this is usually achieved by measuring the distance from the lens to the actor and then adjusting the focus accordingly. If the actor is moving, the focus puller might put tape markers along the floor to indicate the distance. On a video shoot, the focus puller can often see the camera's viewfinder on his own monitor, sometimes operating the lens by remote-control.

Foley Artist: Also known as "footstep men," they add extra ambient sound effects to film by acting along with the edited film which is projected on the wall. They use a variety of props to get the sounds that might not have been picked up on set, for example, small sections of floor devoted to gravel, sod, marble, or wood for making the sounds of footsteps.

Gain: The amplification of an electrical signal. This amplification raises the whole level of that signal, so while the voices on a recording will become louder, the noise of the recording will also become louder. The gain of a video signal can be adjusted as well for extra brightness, but video noise then becomes more apparent.

Gaffer: Chief lighting technician and head of the electrical department. The gaffer handles all lights and lighting crew, and is responsible for the technical security and stability of the entire lighting rig.

Gaffer's Tape: This is what holds film sets and productions schedules together. Even more useful than duct tape, because it has a matte finish, is available in black and white (for marking), and leaves no gluey residue behind. Cloth-based, strong, and doesn't melt on hot lights. It tends to be used extravagantly on most sets to create temporary fixes and solutions to prop and lighting challenges.

Gel: A sheet of tinted transparent plastic used to change the color of the lights. Available in different color registrations and densities, they may also be put over windows to darken the outside light, making interior lighting easier. Gels are heat-resistant so they don't melt and are usually clipped to a light's barn doors with wooden clothespins.

Generation: Refers to how many times the tape has been duplicated, or dubbed, from the original. With each passing generation, some quality is lost. With the advent of digital compression, some formats are advertised as preventing "generation loss" entirely. This is only true if the digital compression format is not changed (decompressed and then recompressed, a process known as transcoding). Every change of media in format or codec means another generation removed from the original material.

Grips: Grips are primarily attached to the camera department. Their first responsibility is to make sure that dolly track is laid, camera mounts are stable, and everything for the shot is in place. The key grip works directly with the DP and the camera team to figure out how to get certain shots, and the rest of the grips are also on hand to help the gaffer and electrical team with light rigging.

Green Light: Usually refers to when a script becomes a film deal and gets final approval to proceed to production. Generally happens after a final budget has been completed.

Gobo: A prop designed to be hung in front of a light so that it casts an interesting shadow, such as a few branches, to give the effect of the sun or moon shining through trees. Other gobos may just be random shapes cut out of styrofoam to break up light and make the shadows more visually interesting. These are sometimes called "cookies" and the light itself may be called the gobo.

Halogen Light: The most common type of light on a film set, available in different amperages and intensities. The color temperature is close to 3200K, making it correct for indoor exposures. The bulbs are very sensitive to the oils on human skin, so they should be changed with gloves.

HDCAM: The HD version of Sony's Betacam tape series, recently updated to HDCAM SR, which can record a full 10-bit 4:4:4 HSDSI signal at 440 or 880 megabits per second. HDCAM is growing in popularity among broadcasters as the standard HD recording media, and is also used for Sony's line of CineAlta cameras, such as their F900 and F950.

HD DVD: An optical disc designed primarily by Toshiba and supported by a number of other manufacturers including Sanyo and Microsoft. It can hold 30 gigabytes of data on two layers, and supports a maximum data transfer rate of 36 megabits per second at 1x speed. As in the VHS vs Betamax format war of the 80s, the influence of the pornography industry may be considerable in deciding a clear market leader, and most adult film studios are supporting HD DVD.

HDTV (High Definition Television): The new standard of television broadcast. First tried in Japan and only now taking off in the U.S., there are several different formats and standards of gear used. The most common are 1080p, which is 1920x1080 and 60 progressive frames per second, 1080i, which is 1920x1080 or 1440x1080 and 30 frames (interlaced 60 fields) per second, and 720p, which is 1280x720 and 60 progressive frames per second. All HD video has an aspect ratio of 16:9.

HDV: A highly compressed video format that puts HD video on a regular DV or miniDV tape. Developed by Sony and JVC, HDV uses an MPEG-2 codec to squeeze a 1080i or 720p video signal onto a 25 megabit per second video tape. This higher compression results in a loss of color data with 4:2:0 subsampling, and introduces motion artifacts since MPEG-2 records image data across multiple frames, instead of on individual frames like DV's MJPEG codec.

HDTV (High Definition Television)**:** The new standard of television broadcast. First tried in Japan and only now taking off in the U.S., there are several different formats and standards of gear used. The most common are 1080i, which is 1920x1080 and 30 frames (interlaced 60 fields) per second, and 720p, which is 1280x720 and 60 progressive frames per second.

Heat: Expressed interest from the filmmaking community. If enough heat can be generated, it might be possible to initiate a bidding war between studios or distributors for rights to a script, project, individual, or finished film.

Hi-8: An improved version of the 8mm camcorder tape format. Hi-8 cameras shoot reasonable resolution images, but they are still not broadcast quality. Sony introduced the Digital8 format using the same tape for a better image, but was not as successful as the higher-quality DV format.

High Concept: An idea that sounds appealing, particularly from a commercial point of view, but also one that is unique. Man-eating lizards chase screaming high-school vacationers through a jungle: low concept. Genetically-cloned dinosaurs chase a child-hating archeologist and a couple of kids through a haywire jungle theme park when corporate espionage goes wrong: high concept.

High Hat: A board or piece of plywood with a tripod head bolted to it. This allows the camera to be placed very low, for dramatic effect. The plywood can be weighted with sandbags, making the tripod head fairly stable, which allows the camera to be placed quickly on a number of surfaces. This highly mobile shooting platform is handy for guerrilla filmmakers.

HMI: A very large, bright light. Their color temperature is balanced to be similar to natural sunlight, about 5400K, so they can be very useful in mixed lighting conditions.

Inciting Incident: The event at the beginning of the film that kicks off the main story. This action will be toward the end of Act I, setting into motion the central plot of the film.

Indie: Slang term for independent. Can mean any person, project, or company that operates independently from the recognized industry leaders. It is now common to hear about Indie record labels, bands, video games, film producers, and filming communities. It has become as all-inclusive and impossible to define as the word "blog."

Insert: Similar to a cutaway; it is specifically a shot within a scene that conveys some special information, such as a close-up of a clock or computer screen, and gives the audience some new data.

Iris: The adjustable aperture at the back of the camera lens which controls how much light hits the film or imaging sensor. It has anywhere from four to twelve metal blades that open, much like the iris in the human eye. The measurement for the iris opening is the f-stop. The wider the iris is opened, the shorter the depth of field and the wider the "circle of confusion" becomes.

Jib Arm: A camera mount that is basically a small crane. The camera is on one end and the controls are on the other, and it pivots around the tripod head. It can drop the camera to the ground, or lift it up to twenty feet in the air. Almost all jib arms are called "Jimmy Jibs" after the most popular brand. A heavy tripod is needed to prevent bounce.

Light Meter: A tool used by the DP and gaffers to measure the light on set. The light meter can give a reading in a number of formats, including f-stops based on what speed of film is being used. A reflected-light meter is held by the camera and pointed at the subject. Its reading shows how much light there is in the scene reflected from the subject. A spot meter follows the same principle, but sees only a tiny spot of that reflected light at a time, rather than the whole scene. An incident-light meter is held next to the subject and pointed back at the camera to measure how much light is illuminating the subject.

Line Producer: A largely accounting-based role. The line producer must be very familiar with all aspects of the day-to-day production operation. However, his main task is to create and approve the budgets. There are generally several of line producers, and they also monitor the production to make sure that the production goals are met within budget.

Location Scout: The person who searches for locations suitable for filming. Sources filming permissions and site access information. A scout might also serve as a location manager, transport organizer, or safety officer during production.

Log Line: The short, usually one-sentence description of a story. Used to explain the basic idea behind a script. Should be twenty-five words or less.

Looping: When a piece of footage is played over and over. Often logos or graphics have looped backgrounds. Some ambient sound effects are looped.

MII: Panasonic's answer to the BetaSP format. It is possible to find MII gear available for very low prices, and it is capable of capturing and storing a high-quality image, but it is also very difficult to find anyone supporting it technically. BetaSP won the standards war against MII, and now digital technology is developing yet newer standards.

Makeup Department: The team that ensures that the actors achieve the look designated by the script and director under specific lighting conditions. This might be simple powder and base application for the leading roles, or prosthetic orc masks for an army of extras. The department is also responsible for continuity of look over days or hours of shooting in challenging conditions.

Mark: Usually a small piece of gaffer's tape placed on the ground to show an actor where to stand so that he is in shot and in focus. Sometimes a "toe bag" is used instead of tape; this is a small beanbag the actor can feel with his feet and thus hit his marks without looking down. A mark may also refer to the frame of the clapper coming together.

Matte Box: The square box that sits on the front of the lens. It shades the lens from indirect light that might cause lens flares and glare, and holds any filters that might be needed to alter the captured image prior to processing or editing. Sometimes a hand-cut matte will be inserted to block a part of the field of view, so special effects can be added over the unexposed portion of the film. This was more common in the days of optically printed effects, but is still done.

Mixing Desk: Refers to a control board used for mixing either video or audio signals. A video mixer, or switcher, is most often used in live television production, where a number of feeds from studio cameras can be fed into the mixer simultaneously and the program director can switch from one camera to another. Most video switchers also have some limited transitional effects and the ability to overlay certain graphics.

Montage: A series of shots that condense a string of actions into a short scene. It should be used sparingly because, like the voice over, even though it conveys a lot of information very quickly, it tends to pull the audience out of the story in order to present it to them.

Moviola: A special desk for editing film. It has a bright light that projects the image up onto a small, ground glass screen, which stands between two reels of film, which can be manually rolled forward and backward past the light, with a crank on each reel. The film is cut with a small guillotine and spliced together with tape. Still in use for some film editing. Larger versions with motorized reels are referred to as "flatbeds."

MPEG: One of the first digital video codecs, and now its own file format. MPEG existed primarily to squeeze video into a much smaller size, and is only now of a high enough quality to be used for production. MPEG2 is the format used to encode DVDs, and in slightly different configurations, DV and HDV formats. MPEG4 is a lower quality, higher compression codec usually used over the Internet.

Noise: Electronic signal interference. Video noise is seen as a fuzzy, snowy image, and audio noise is a hiss or a hum. Sometimes a technician can tell from the type of noise where the interference is coming from.

Non-Linear Editing: The organizing of digitized images on a computer program by arranging short scenes or "clips" in a non-destructive way, much like cutting and pasting words and paragraphs in a word processing program. It offers a number of advantages over linear tape editing or moviola editing including an almost unlimited number of video and audio tracks and the ability to jump instantly to any point in a project or clip without fast-forwarding or rewinding the original tape or film stock.

NTSC: The National Television Standards Committee's standard for color TV broadcasting, used mainly in the United States, Canada, Mexico, and Japan. Its full, digital frame size is 720x486 and runs at 29.97 frames per second, interlaced, but this is usually rounded up to 30fps.

On the Nose: Dialogue that expresses precisely what a character is feeling with no subterfuge. It is rare that this style of dialogue will work in a final scene, but in early drafts characters can speak on the nose until the writer knows their motivation.

Option: The exclusive rights to a script or literary property, but only for a set amount of time. Studios or producers generally option scripts so that they have complete control over the project while they research its viability. At the end of this time period, the rights revert back to the original owner, and he can option the script to another studio if the first decides not to produce it.

P2: A tapeless video format designed by Panasonic for news gathering purposes. Unlike Sony's optical XDCAM system, the P2 cards use faster solid state memory chips which can plug directly into a modern laptop. Unfortunately, P2 cards are expensive and have a very limited recording capacity - $2,000 for 16gb at the time of this writing. At present the P2 system uses only the DCVPRO codec family.

Pace: The speed and rhythm of the story. The writer sets the pace of the script, and it is honed for the final film in shooting and editing.

Package: Whatever can be attached to a script to make it more valuable when pitched to investors or studios. This generally refers to actors, directors, producers, usually put together by an agent hired by the writer. This package is usually a combination of talent and material that has been chosen to interest a large studio. An independent filmmaker could add anything to his package; location details, executive producers, and preliminary funding in order to have the leverage required to negotiate a co-production.

PAL (Phase Alternate Line): The European color TV broadcasting standard, which is 720x576 and runs at 25 frames per second, interlaced. In addition to more vertical resolution, it handles some extreme colors slightly better than NTSC.

Pan: When the camera swings from to the left or right, but rotates on the tripod head instead of moving on a dolly.

Panavision Genesis: A high-end digital cinema camera built by Panavision to take advantage of existing Panavision accessories and lenses. It has a full 35mm imaging chip, and shoot variable-speed 4:4:4 HD images at 10-bit color depth. At the time of this writing it is the dominant digital cinema camera that has been used for studio films, having shot *Superman Returns, Flyboys, Apocalypto,* and several other big-budget films.

Pitch: The verbal description of the story or script meant to sell it. You should have several well-polished pitches of different lengths; the ten-minute pitch for long meetings, the five-minute pitch for short meetings, and the thirty-second pitch for people that you bump into.

Premise: The question that best describes the most basic idea of the plot, such as, "What if scientists could clone dinosaurs from ancient DNA?"

Producer: Usually the main boss, overseeing and delegating the hiring of talent, crew, equipment. The sole authority over contracts, permits, and anything else necessary to complete the project. Producers deal more with the business aspect of making movies, enabling the director to focus on directing.

Production Management: Or Unit Production Manager. Helps the producer with budgets, shooting schedules, locations, permissions, etc. Solely involved in principal photography.

Property Master: Or Propmaster. Responsible for all props needed for a shoot. He may have to design props from scratch and have them built and delivered, or he could find and hire them. On some productions, the Propmaster is the armorer and responsible for prop weapons; but this might also be under the authority of the practical effects team.

Protagonist: The hero whose every action and ultimate goal drive the plot forward.

Rack Focus: When the camera suddenly or slowly changes focus from foreground to background or vice versa. Useful for changing the audience's center of attention in a single shot.

RED ONE: The first digital cinema camera scheduled to be released by Jim Jannard's new camera company. Touted as a cheap replacement for expensive film cameras, its original $17,500 price does not included lenses, lens adapters, viewfinder, rails, handles, batteries, battery mounts, or even any way to record footage. Despite the expense of a complete package, it does shoot beautiful 4k imagery and has a reportedly well-planned workflow for acquiring and balancing images.

Remote Head: A robotic head the camera is mounted on enabling it to be operated from elsewhere. These are used on gyroscopic camera mounts on helicopters, or on certain light cranes. Heavy-duty cranes might lift the camera operator as well as the camera.

Rigging: The technical aspect of filmmaking. Rigging is the placement of lights, set pieces, camera equipment, certain props, markers for actors or effects, etc.

Rolling Shutter: Most CCD cameras have a frame shutter, which captures the entire frame image at exactly the same time while the shutter is "open," similar to how a film camera's shutter works. However, many cheaper CMOS cameras have a rolling shutter, where every line of resolution is captured at a different time. This is problematic because it causes fast-moving objects to shear or wobble, and even slow pans can distort the entire frame.

Script Supervisor: Similar to the continuity person; or on a smaller production possibly also the continuity person. Keeps a copy of the script on hand and notes any changes in dialogue, shot angles, props, or anything else that may have changed from what is printed in the shooting script. Also keeps general notes on takes and performance that the director might find useful when filming adjacent scenes.

SDTV (Standard Definition Television): SD is a recently-coined retronym referring to all non-HD video resolutions.

Second Unit: A smaller counterpart to the main filming unit. Shoots scenes that the main cast are not involved with, such as certain stunts or effects plates, or background establishing shots. They essentially handle everything that the director doesn't need personal control over. The second unit director still needs to understand the director's vision.

Slate: The part of the clapperboard that scene information is written on. The clapper is used to synchronize the audio, and the slate is used by the editor to find certain scenes and good takes in a roll of film. Some new slates have LCD timecode readouts that are synced to computerized shot logging software for better tracking.

SMPTE Timecode: The Society of Motion Picture and Television Engineers' standard for storing and displaying timecode. Each frame has its own unique address which shows up as "hours:minutes:seconds:frames." A professional camera will allow you to set the timecode that a tape uses, so you can shoot five hours of footage and set all your tapes to display those five hours concurrently. This will allow you to find footage on the tapes quickly and easily.

Sound Mixer: The technician responsible for capturing sound on set. He runs the mixer feeding the sound recorder, chooses microphone types to be used, and directs the boom operator on how to get the best sound.

Sound Stage: A completely controlled environment for shooting, housed in a large building with plenty of room for set construction. It should have soundproofing on the walls and ceiling, a lighting grid wired for a huge number of lights, cranes for moving set pieces and camera gear, and other production tools that may not be available on location.

Spec Script: Any script written without some prior guarantee that it will have a buyer—written with the speculation that it might sell. Nearly all scripts are spec scripts, and most film production offices are overflowing with submitted scripts.

Special Effects: There are usually two separate effects teams; the practical effects team which works on set during principle photography, and the visual effects team which creates elements to be added to the film later in post-production. Both groups are overseen by the effects supervisor. The practical team sets explosives, rigs car wrecks, sets up snowstorms, and helps the stunt department with certain things. The post team will build miniature sets if needed, handle the compositing of effects elements, and add computer animation.

Spot Meter: A special type of light meter that specifically measures the amount of reflective light coming off an object. It is used in conjunction with a regular light meter to give the DP a more precise idea of how much light is in a scene and how much is bouncing off of a specific object back into the camera.

Spreader: Either a loop of rope or a rigid three-legged tool that attaches to the bottom of a tripod's legs to keep them from spreading out too far. Also called a spider.

Stand-Ins: People roughly the same size as the main actors, and sometimes chosen for a similar complexion. Usually there for lighting purposes so lights can be rigged before the cast arrives.

Steadicam: A spring-loaded arm attached to a special harness that the camera can be attached to. It is specially balanced and counterweighted to eliminate any shaky movement. The steadicam operator must be practiced in its use because of its weight and awkward balance. Several manufacturers build spring arm stabilizers commonly referred to as "Steadicams," but the best are made by Tiffen Steadicam, the original inventor.

Synopsis: A one-half to two-page description of a script or story. A written pitch, describing the plot and characters

Sticks: Tripod legs.

Take: One uninterrupted camera shot. Depending on the requirements of the script and the plans of the director, takes may be simple or highly complex. Each take requires the synchronized cooperation of many technicians and actors. The director must decide if and when a usable take is successfully captured to film. It typically requires several tries to accomplish a successful take.

Telecine: A machine that transfers film to video. Used for putting dailies onto tape or converting film masters onto distribution material. Film that is digitized for special effects or post processing must be scanned at a much higher resolution, which requires different gear.

Teleprompter: A devices that uses a two-way mirror to allow the talent to read his lines off a scrolling computer screen mounted below the camera while still looking directly into the camera lens. Used by news anchors and talk show hosts.

Tilt: Pivoting the camera up and down on the tripod head. Similar to a pan.

Too Much Black: The way script pages with too much description are often described. The very format of scripts allows basic pacing to be judged at a glance. It is simple to see how long most lines of dialogue are, and how complex each scene is to set up. It is important to be efficient and concise.

Tracking Shot: A shot where the camera follows a character or action, either using a dolly or a Steadicam.

Trade Papers: The daily periodicals reporting on the latest projects, deals, and events within the film business. The two most popular are *Variety* and *Hollywood Reporter*.

Treatment: A summary of the way a film would be handled, containing information about the style, story content, genre, plot, characters, and directorial approach. Hollywood treatments are usually submitted in one, four, and twelve-page formats. A "log-line" is a one or two-sentence description of a film; a synopsis is usually a paragraph or two long. A writer should write two versions of the treatment; the first should be written before the script and used as a tool to flesh out the scenes and plot points, and the second should be written later as a pitch or sales tool.

Tripod Head: The connection between camera and tripod legs. The head allows the camera to be panned back and forth and tilted up and down. Some special heads allow for "Dutch angles" where the camera is tilted to the side, setting the horizon at an angle. High-quality heads contain some sort of viscous lubricating fluid for extra smooth operation.

Twist: Or "False Ending." An unexpected story point, usually half-way into the third act. A good twist introduces new circumstances, but no new story elements, and should be tied directly into the plot and theme of the film. See *War Games* for a good example of a twist that raises the stakes and remains relative to the story.

U-Matic: An old 3/4" tape format. It was introduced in 1971 but is capable of producing acceptable broadcast images. Difficult to support, was replaced by Betacam.

Vectorscope: A diagnostic tool that allows the chroma in a video signal to be examined in a very precise way. It shows where each pixel of the image is on a color wheel (hue) and how strong each color is (saturation). This can be used for exact color corrections in post, and to calibrate certain gear.

VHS: The most common form of consumer videotape. It is not broadcast quality and deteriorates rapidly with age and concurrent generations. However, it is so widespread that it is still useful for showing demo or test material. S-VHS is slightly higher quality and carries embedded timecode.

Viper Filmstream: A digital cinema camera made by Thompson Grass Valley. It captures images on three 1920x1080 and sends unprocessed 12-bit 4:4:4 video out uncompressed to a tape deck or to Grass Valley's proprietary Venom disk recorder. It is known for its excellent low-light performance and has been used in the productions of *Collateral, Zodiac,* and *Miami Vice.*

Vox Pops: Short, snappy, impromptu man-on-the-street interviews. Short for *vox populi*, Latin for "the voice of the people."

Waveform Monitor: A diagnostic tool that allows the luminance of a video signal to be examined in a very precise way. The levels of white, black, and separate colors can be measured by displaying the luminosity of an image on the monitor along a vertical scale. For measuring the strength of video signals and testing the exposure of image.

White Balance: An internal computer function on a video camera to calibrate color balance to the natural spectrum under any lighting condition. In the field it should be done any time lighting conditions change, typically by pointing camera at a white object and "manually" running the camera through the calibration process. Consumer cameras generally only have an automatic white balance, which is usually less effective. Some directors will white balance on a slightly blue card to give their footage a warmer look.

Wrylies: The parenthetical cues placed in a script before lines of dialogue, which describe how the character speaks. To be used only when the speaker's emotive state isn't obvious from his actions in the scene.

XDCAM: Sony's optical disc-based video system for SD and HD video recording. Designed specifically for electronic news gathering and television production, the XDCAM "Professional disc" is based on the Blu-ray disc and can record almost 24 gigabytes of data at up to 88 megabits per second. The system can use a variety of codecs including DigiBeta's IMX, MPEG-2 and 4, and regular DV, and can record a total of eight separate audio channels. The discs are cheap (at the time of this writing about $30 each), light, and durable, making them ideal for journalists and documentary filmmakers. They may also have some value an archival media.

Appendix D.

INDEX

P

R

S

INDEX

INDEX